Out of the Fog

3 Books in 1:

A Guide to a Narcissist Victim, Healing From Narcissist Emotional Abuse and Emotionally Immature Parents.

Gloria Newton

Legal & Disclaimer

The information contained in this book and its contents is not designed to replace or take the place of any form of medical or professional advice; and is not meant to replace the need for independent medical, financial, legal or other professional advice or services, as may be required. The content and information in this book has been provided for educational and entertainment purposes only.

The content and information contained in this book has been compiled from sources deemed reliable, and it is accurate to the best of the Author's knowledge, information and belief. However, the Author cannot guarantee its accuracy and validity and cannot be held liable for any errors and/or omissions. Further, changes are periodically made to this book as and when needed. Where appropriate and/or necessary, you must consult a professional (including but not limited to your doctor, attorney, financial advisor or such other professional advisor) before using any of the suggested remedies, techniques, or information in this book.

Upon using the contents and information contained in this book, you agree to hold harmless the Author from and against any damages, costs, and expenses, including any legal fees potentially resulting from the application of any of the information provided by this book. This disclaimer applies to any loss, damages or injury caused by the use and application, whether directly or indirectly, of any advice or information presented, whether for breach of contract, tort, negligence, personal injury, criminal intent, or under any other cause of action.

You agree to accept all risks of using the information presented inside this book.

You agree that by continuing to read this book, where appropriate and/or necessary, you shall consult a professional (including but not limited to your doctor, attorney, or financial advisor or such other advisor as needed) before using any of the suggested remedies, techniques, or information in this book.

Table of Contents

A GUIDE TO A NARCISSIST VICTIM

HEALING FROM NARCISSIST EMOTIONAL ABUSE

Emotionally Immature Parents

A GUIDE TO A NARCISSIST VICTIM

HOW TO FIND PERSONALITY DISORDER AND DEAL WITH A NARCISSIST IN MARRIAGE, AT WORKPLACE AND IN YOUR DAILY LIFE

[Gloria Newton]

INTRODUCTION

It is important that people learn and become aware of this disorder. People should realize that this is one of the most significant personality disorders. It is a mental condition that makes a person lack empathy towards others, have troubled relationships, have a great need for excessive admiration and attention. These are people who put on a mask at all time to hide their true identity. It is agreed that narcissists have delicate self-esteem that is vulnerable to even a little criticism. Generally, they are unhappy people and do not feel emotions like remorse or real love. They tend to imagine and pretend to have these feelings. They construct an ideology; have strategies and plans about to win a person, which makes them better during the first stages of a relationship. They are able to study their victims and learn their strengths and weaknesses. That is why it is difficult for a narcissist to engage with a person that they realize lacks weaknesses or strengths that they can exploit.

You are not the only victim of a narcissist - millions of others have found themselves in the same situation. There are narcissists everywhere, at the workplace at school or anywhere you find a grouping of people. While both genders are affected, females tend to be the victims in this who suffer more. More women are physically abused as compared to men. By nature, women are empathic which makes them more vulnerable.

Because most people do not realize this, they then spend years of their lives in these relationships and in trying to make it work. It is so unfortunate that by the time one has realized that there is nothing they can do to make their partners happy; it is too late, and they have wasted a tremendous period of their life.

A narcissist is a person who has a personality disorder in which he or she is excessively preoccupied with dominance, power, prestige, and vanity. They do not realize the destruction they cause to themselves and others. A so-called narcissist can do things without noticing the feelings of the people around them. They consider themselves truly superior and they need to be respected. You can call them vain or selfish, those are just some of the common labels used by many towards narcissists. They are involved in feelings, as for them it's only normal to feel hurt. They came up with this **narcissist** version of themselves so that it can serve as the shock absorber.

However, a narcissistic pain is different from other types of emotional pain. People who suffer from narcissism often display attitudes like being snobbish, patronizing or even disdain. For example, he or she may complain about a bartender's rudeness or stupidity or conclude a medical evaluation with a condescending evaluation of the physician.

A personality disorder is a kind of pattern and behavior that deviates from the norm individual's culture. This pattern is seen in the following areas: cognition; interpersonal functioning;

impulse control; or affect. The enduring pattern is not exactly flexible and it can also be seen at one's early childhood characteristics. The pattern is stable and is in long duration.

There are actually treatments of this personality disorder, which typically involves long-term psycho treatment or psychotherapy, with a therapist who has a wide experience in treating this kind of personality disorder. Some medications can actually help with specific sets of symptoms. The person with this kind of disorder usually exaggerate things around him, they also tend to have a daydreaming about fantasies of beauty, success and power over dominating their thoughts. This type of person is also too sensitive. They need to be admired in everything they do at all times. If not, they will be hurt deep inside.

They also tend to manipulate and take advantage of the people around them using their emotional feelings that people around them needs to consider, as a weapon. They lack empathy that makes us feel and recognize the feelings of needs of others. These types of people also are the envy type ones and their behavior appears to us as haughty or arrogant.

Worst cases can turn a human being to someone who is very abusive both physically and sexually. Living with a narcissist can feel as if you're living a very confusing nightmare. It's like you are getting into jail with a no exact way of escape. The spouse, co-workers, boss, and even the parent can sometimes get stuck in a relationship they find very hard to escape from. The emotional and the physical damages caused by somebody with the disorder can be severe. Health care professionals aren't an exception to emotional exhaustion.

They fear their feelings. They cannot gain and keep a deep friendship or intimacy and cannot develop a mature love relationship. A fantasy world can be a sweet escape for a narcissist and can also become an attempt not to see what is really there in order to build up self-esteem. Narcissist people process information, emotions, and unresolved pain to make up for their hidden damaged childhood. They love achieving something with their own imaginations in their created world and they often place an unrealistic demand to someone else just to feel better. They are not one to tolerate negative emotional distress, as they are not very good at it. They usually push it to others and blame them instead of looking closer to see their own part of the problem. This is the defense of projection – when a certain person does not like him or herself, they get angry to those who have some of the likable traits.

The Self-image is distorted in narcissistic point of view and the person believes that he is more superior than others. An over the top self-esteem is a defense to cover up the unforgettable shame deep within. Grandiosity is an insidious error in thinking that it is a prevention and it stops them from blaming themselves and becoming depressed or disintegrated.

Narcissist people like to hear the sound of their own voice. They are individuals that thrive on being the center of attraction and attention who tends to put down others whom they feel is inferior. At work, a narcissist is power hungry and will go to great lengths to gain power. Learning if you are with a narcissist can be quite difficult and confusing in the sense that you also might be confused about what you feel towards the narcissist you are with.

Narcissists prefer to work under their own set of rules. Narcissist only cares about themselves and therefore, when working with a narcissist, always remember that they will never be a great buddy to be with. They will befriend you to convert you into one of their victims or supply sources, will do favors expecting a big return and you will do the same thing as well to them. Unfortunately, in the workplace you can't just do anything that you want to this person and walk away without so much as an issue. So the best thing to do is to go along with him or her. Getting in touch with a narcissist more often will keep them from thinking you don't like them. But be careful of getting too close with a narcissist because they think different and digest words from you differently. Narcissist do expect you to be immediately responsive the moment they demand attention just like a normal boss in your company who wants you to immediately follow him in everything he demands.

Sharing your emotions to a narcissist is a big no because you are forcing them to prioritize your feelings. The next best thing that you can actually do is focus on solutions and not the problem. Narcissist likes to focus on the problem and turn it over, around, rearrange, and practically dissect it to pieces. They tend to make things very complicated. Stop looking at the glass as if it is half empty. The best thing that you can do is flip it and influence the narcissist to see the other side of truth.

It's actually a good choice to just present several solutions. Narcissist likes to be in control and they'd love you if you have this much-favored ability to offer them options. This is one of the several ways that you can make them feel as if you truly respect their opinion and that you are asking them to take control and show you what they are made of. If it still does not work out, you best last option is to make them feel good about themselves, unique, and special. Narcissists wants to be praised and they like the feeling that they are higher than you. They get high off of being in power and they thrive in attention and admiration. If you want them to be happily productive for you, simply let them know how great they are. Praising them makes them feel at peace.

When a narcissist grows up, they harbor the irrational belief that the person they choose as a partner will give them perfect love and make up for all hurts and slights of their life. This burning desire for getting unconditional love is an unresolved need from their damaged childhood. While most adults find the good thing about unconditional, understand also that it rarely happens. This is because the people we love usually holding us somehow responsible for our actions. Think carefully about imposing your neediness and bad behavior towards others.

CHAPTER 1: NARCISSIST AND ITS TYPES

NPD is by no means a one-size-fits-all diagnosis. It is a spectrum. Some narcissists are more harmful and toxic while others are somewhat harmless. Some narcissists are obvious, and others are more subtle. Understanding the differences between these varying kinds of narcissism is key for understanding how each should be handled.

LIST OF ALL TYPES

Vulnerable Narcissist

Vulnerable or covert narcissists are typically more sensitive than their grandiose counterparts. Vulnerable narcissists are so caught up in fearing rejection or abandonment that they constantly swing between feelings superior to those around them to inferior based upon what is happening at the moment. During times of inferiority, they seek validation from others in order to boost their egos. Oftentimes, these narcissists are hiding their low self-esteem; projecting a persona of the victim. The vulnerable narcissist is always the victim, always demanding sympathy, and always seeking to make those around them see them as perfect. They often appear as quiet and calm, though they also struggle with emotional regulation.

Behind their narcissistic mask lies a person so broken, ashamed, and self-conscious that they put on a front to pretend to the world that they are perfect. These people seem to be overcompensating for their negative feelings and less-than-stellar view of self-worth, often due to trauma suffered in early childhood. Just like the other forms of narcissists, people who develop this form of NPD often do as a coping mechanism to handle any neglect, abuse, or trauma they faced as children. They develop a persona that is perfect, always fixating on doing things exactly right. If they are perfect, they can deny that anything bad that happens is their fault and they can develop an identity encompassed in a victim mentality. They crave the attachment or love they lacked had as children, and fears the abandonment they faced so much that they will do anything to garner the sympathy needed to keep people nearby.

These people care greatly about how those around them perceive them and will go out of their way to build rapport, and even apologize if they think it will get them the desired results. They pride themselves on being seen as outstanding members of their society, but every good deed they do is solely to continue being seen as perfect and receiving the admiration and attention that goes hand in hand with doing good deeds. These are the people who will only do something selfless or generous if there is an audience, or will always, without fail, post their good deeds on social media for people to see. They are more likely to aim for very public careers that leave them engaging with people on the regular, usually in a context where they provide aid to others, as this feeds their need for attention, and also make them appear to be great, upstanding people.

Unlike most of those with personality disorders, vulnerable narcissists are one of the only people who will make threats to harm themselves in order to get attention from those around them, though they will rarely follow through with their threat. These people seek sympathy through any means necessary to get their narcissistic supply, and because of this, they are often emotionally draining. They demand plenty of emotional investment while being quite sensitive as well, making those around them walk on eggshells out of fear of setting off the vulnerable narcissist.

When threatened, the vulnerable narcissist will become quite passive aggressive, as it is never his fault something went wrong. He will passive-aggressively shut out those that threaten him, with comments such as a dejected, "Well, if I am such a big bother, I'll just never go out of my way to talk to you again," fishing for you to either try to convince him that he should stay with you and that you want him there and in his life, or to agree with him, which gives him more material to use to play the victim and garner sympathy from others. When challenges continue, the vulnerable narcissist is much more explosive than the grandiose narcissist, internalizing the feelings and lashing out.

The more vulnerable the narcissist, the more explosive the aggressive will become. As these people already have poor self-esteem, any threat to it is incredibly provocative.

Vulnerable narcissists pride themselves on being a great parent, child, sibling, spouse or whatever else they identify themselves as. For those who live with the narcissist, they likely often hear people say they are so lucky to have the narcissist in their lives, and the person is stuck feeling confused; no one is ever good enough for the narcissist, and the narcissist will be sure to make that clear. Growing up with a narcissistic parent, the child is constantly told he is lucky, but at home, he is constantly criticized. The end result is the child believing that he must be the problem if everyone else thinks his parents are fantastic. This is just the beginning of the damage inflicted by narcissists; the child starts life with a deep-seated belief that there is something inherently wrong with him.

Grandiose Narcissist

Unlike the vulnerable narcissist, the grandiose variety knows that he is better than everyone else and is unafraid of acting as such. These people are much less sensitive than the vulnerable narcissists and do not care as much about what other people think. They are confident, loud, and have high self-esteem, even if it is unwarranted. They are always the hero of every story, and anyone that ever wrongs them is obviously wrong. For the grandiose narcissist, if someone thinks he is less than stellar or disagrees with his stance on something, obviously that person is a plebeian that is too stupid to understand and appreciate genius, and therefore, their opinion means nothing. Anything that critic says will be disregarded as unimportant and untrue.

Likewise, in relationships, the grandiose narcissist does not care if his partner likes him. He does not care about his partner at all, only seeking to use the other person until they are no longer useful. If his partner does not admire and respect him in the way he is so confident he deserves just by virtue of being the perfect, most important, most superior person he knows, he is willing to drop everything and move on to the next victim. He also may have a penchant for indiscreetly carrying multiple affairs, not caring when his primary partner discovers the truth. In fact, he may also accuse his partner of being the one having affairs, or even get angry at his partner when called out.

These narcissists are loud about their achievements, domineering, oftentimes aggressive about getting what they want, and have no qualms about using and hurting people to get what they know they deserve. They brag about every little success that makes them appear better than those they speak to, oftentimes putting down the listener at the same time. The grandiose narcissist will not apologize, even if it will make him look better because he does not care about other people. In his mind, apologizing is something only equals or superiors deserve, and since he is obviously the best person, those he wrongs do not deserve anything.

In contrast with the vulnerable narcissist, who is overcompensating by creating a persona to garner attention and sympathy to validate her self-worth, the grandiose narcissist is not compensating for anything. He is acting on his belief and expectation that he is superior, and he should be treated as such. He may have been told throughout his entire childhood that he is superior to those around him or treated better due to social status or intelligence, and he comes to expect that treatment to carry over into every aspect of his life. He could have been top in his class or the varsity football captain and treated like royalty in school, and he held the expectation that that admiration would follow him for the rest of his life.

The grandiose narcissist thinks that if he believes something, it will become true, regardless of how disordered the thought process is. He will absolutely find some illogical way to justify his beliefs, and he will absolutely believe it. Like children, who will try to wish things into reality, the grandiose narcissist will believe their desires will happen. In their minds, there is absolutely no possible way they are wrong. If you try to provide evidence to support the fact they are wrong, they will brush you off, claiming that what you say is little more than opinion, and deny it has any plausibility. He will also do anything in his power in order to defend his belief and make his desires come true.

They will not take no for an answer and will go to extreme lengths to get what they want.

Interestingly, despite grandiose narcissists believing they are much better than everyone else and expecting things to go their way, they are much more flexible when dealing with conflict. Where the vulnerable narcissist erupts into a rage at things not going as expected, the grandiose narcissist makes what he wants to happen. The grandiose narcissist will exploit and manipulate anything necessary in order to get the results he wants; even if that means upholding delusional beliefs that something went exactly according to plan. They are as confident in themselves as they present their own view of reality that they convince some people around them to believe the same.

This may be the ex-husband, who cries to everyone about how much he wanted to be involved in his children's lives, but his monster of an ex-wife poisoned their minds and kept them away from him when in reality, he abandoned his children and has been avoiding their calls and attempts at contact. Despite the fact that he abandoned them, he believes wholeheartedly that his spouse alienated his children from him and shifts all of the blame to her. After all, he has always been a fantastic father and his children adored him. Those around him will take his words at face value, unaware that he simply no longer found his children useful now that they were old enough to question him, and he himself will believe the delusions he has declared. These narcissists are so convincing in their manipulation that they even manage to manipulate themselves into believing their delusions.

Malignant Narcissist

While some narcissists are little more than annoying and exhausting to interact with, a small percentage are downright toxic. These are known as malignant narcissists, and they are utterly vicious, destructive, and inhumane. These people teeter somewhere between both NPD and ASPD, often embodying all of the identifying traits of narcissists with some of ASPDs antisocial behavior tendencies, along with sadistic tendencies and, oftentimes, paranoia. These narcissists thrive off of inflicting pain and torment wherever they go.

Described by some as the epitome of evil, these people are the quintessential villain who wants nothing more than to watch the world burn. These people, though they present as grandiose and charming, have a fragile ego and are sensitive to any sort of criticism. They feel an intense desire for recognition, and they envy those around them that have the success they desire. They work hard to achieve success and present themselves as successful, though this is solely to get the admiration they desire. In reality, however, deep within themselves, they feel crushing self-doubt, inferiority, and emptiness, and they feel paranoid that their true selves will be discovered, or even worse, that others are actively seeking to expose them.

These narcissists are outwardly charming and sometimes promiscuous or seductive, but despite this gravitation toward physical intimacy with others, they are unable to develop any truly meaningful relationship. Any relationship pursued is for their own self-interest, and when they have satisfied whatever desire they had, they suddenly shift to cold and apathetic toward whoever was being used.

As seen in antisocial personality disorder, the malignant narcissist vehemently dislikes social conventions, and as such, tends to lie and steal. They have a blatant disregard for the law, and may even commit violent crimes or form terrorist organizations. These antisocial tendencies lend themselves to acts of violence or sadism, which is little more than a way of self-affirmation. By hurting and destroying those around him, the malignant narcissist feels gratification. They lack any and all forms of empathy for others, unlike other narcissists, who may feel some reduced capacity of empathy, but are still capable of feeling regret or remorse.

While manipulation is a key feature of all narcissists, those with malignant narcissism are actively seeking to manipulate others, intentionally honing their skills and calculating every move to get exactly what they want. The malignant narcissists are much more forceful in their attempts to manipulate, even if their forcefulness comes with a cost of decreasing how subtle the attempts are. Unlike how many other narcissists' opportunistic manipulation, the malignant narcissist proactively manipulates others, enjoying the process almost as much as enjoying the suffering the victim feels.

Like all narcissists, the malignant narcissists crave attention; this is a vital form of emotional and mental nourishment for them. Unlike other narcissists, however, malignant narcissists have no preference between positive or negative attention. They do not care what other people think about them, so long as other people are actively thinking about them. A negative thought about them is still good enough, and sometimes, these people will intentionally play the villain in order to garner negative attention intentionally.

The malignant narcissist is the most toxic form of narcissism there is, and these people should be avoided if at all possible. They love to cause suffering, reveling in the pain of others. They intentionally inflict harm with no regard for suffering or social conventions and do what they want when they want. These narcissists are dangerous and do not have the mental capacity to keep them from hurting, or even killing, their targets if they desire to do so.

CHAPTER 2: TRAITS OF A NARCISSIST

The definition of a psychopath is a person who suffers from a mental disorder who could manifest violent or abnormal social behavior. They are mainly considered aggressive and unstable, which allows them to cause major mental, emotional, and sometimes even physical abuse on people around them.

If you haven't seen the dark side of your narcissist, it might shock you to learn that the narcissist is a psychopath. They have deep-seated mental issues that likely reach back as far as their childhood. This is why it is pretty much impossible for a person with NPD to recover.

Many in-depth studies of narcissistic and psychopathic behavior have found certain behavioral patterns that they follow. These are tendencies that you are likely going to notices in nearly all narcissists, and many have very similar personalities.

Even though everybody displays narcissistic tendencies from varying degrees, they are not to the point of being labeled a psychopath. Only if these behaviors start to cause abnormalities in social functioning is the person then seen to be a full blown narcissist.

Manipulation

Narcissists have a plethora of manipulation techniques that they can use at any moment. It would take a while to go through every single one, but it is helpful to know them so that you better understand their true self, so we will touch on the more common ones. Once you know those, it's easy to spot the rest. In fact, we've touched on one already, gas lighting.

The first one, and likely the most used, is shaming. This can be in private or in public. The purpose of the shame is often two-fold, and can use a combination of their other techniques. This is something you will likely start to notice is that their tactics will overlap, and the goal of most is to manipulate you to do what they want you to. The two-fold purpose of shaming is, one, to up their own intelligence and worth, and two, to make you feel less than them.

This shaming is used to encourage you to submit to your abuser. This shaming will like thoughts like, "They seem to know more than me, so it might be best for me to take my cues from them and then, maybe, I can deserve their praise," may cross their mind. With this mentality, everything you say and do will be geared towards making sure your abuser is happy and approves, which is exactly what they wanted to achieve.

Another manipulation tactic is playing the role of the victim. This normally starts when the abused is in a spot where they feel inconvenienced by the demands of the narcissist. Here's an example:

Amanda is a little low on cash after her job laid her off since her company had to make budget cuts. She is going into her third month without a job, and she has to turn to friends and family for financial support. She has been asking Brian for some help over the past few weeks, and at first, he was happy to help her out. But now her financial needs are making a noticeable dent in his own finances.

For the umpteenth time, Amanda has asked Brian for some cash, but Brain isn't as willing this time. "If I give you the money I have on hand, I won't be able to cover my bills. I can't help out this time. I hope you understand."

"I can't believe you could treat me this way. I literally have no job and I have to have money in order to survive. But of course, getting "behind" on your own bills is much worse than my problems. Sorry for bothering you."

Brian still gives her the money and says that he will use his next paycheck to catch up on his bills. Was Amanda right to demand what she did from her friend?

First off, Brian is in control of his own finances, so he has the right to choose how he uses his money that he works hard for. Choosing to help Amanda or not is up to him and nobody else should hold his decision against him.

Second, it's important to remember that Amanda has been without a job for three months, which is likely more than enough time to get another job to help her meet her financial needs. The fact that she is choosing to rely on others to help meet her financial needs shows that she is likely enjoying the setup of surviving without having to work for it.

She still manages to manipulate Brian into putting her interests in front of his own by making him feel guilty. She is playing the role of the victim. She highlights her problems and minimizes Brian's to make him come off as greedy and unreasonable.

The next manipulation tactic is conditional love. This manipulation tactic provides the abused with enough affection to make them want to be on their abuser's good side. Narcissists will often use this when the victim makes them happy or does something that makes them look good. It works as positive reinforcement so that the victim wants to continue doing the good work.

Genuine love is supposed to be unconditional. It shouldn't come with strings attached. Real love loves the person despite their shortcomings. Unfortunately, a narcissist is unable to do this.

If their victim does anything that they don't approve of, they will without their affection and love, and will make their victim feel undeserving of their love. It's only after they apology and acknowledge their mistakes that the narcissist will "forgive" them.

The last manipulation tactic we'll talk about is blaming you for everything. They use this to make sure that their image stays clean while making their victim feel accountable for everything. Narcissists never want to appear wrong in any situation, and so they will do whatever it takes to make sure that they never get blamed for anything bad.

They will look for a scapegoat, which will typically be their current victim, and they will turn around the situation to make that person feel bad. This will cause their victim to feel unworthy, which causes them to hold tighter to their abuser out of fear of being alone.

Most of them time, narcissists will also make sure to let others know of the victim's shortcomings. This overly done, with the victim completely aware that other people in their world are aware of the ways they have messed up. This causes the victim to feel embarrassed, and it makes them submit to their abuser to show remorse and a want to correct their mistakes.

All of these different strategies for manipulation don't only make the victim act in a certain fashion in that moment, but it also instills a long-term want to keep the relationship healthy for the foreseeable future. This destroys the victim's free-will and self-worth so that they are reliant on the abuser. This gives the narcissist the ability to control their actions.

What does the narcissist get out of all of this control? Narcissists thrive on praise and admiration. Having people under their spell gives them the ability to get a hit whenever they need it. Their victim's endless need to please them gives then a consistent source of admiration.

On top of this, they also feel like they are entitled to all of this and can use people however they need to. In their mind, they are better than everybody so they have the right to make others feel bad and make the subordinate. By controlling your life, they are helping you out since they think they know better than you do.

The need for attention

Narcissists not only want constant attention but will also demand the same. That behavior can be something as simple as constantly following you around the house, saying outrageous things to grab your attention, or asking you to do things for them. Narcissists' wants for validation is as constant as their need for attention. They require constant validation, and it doesn't count unless it comes from others. Even then, it doesn't mean much.

A narcissist's need for attention and validation is like a black hole that can never be filled. You can channel all your positivity, support, and attention, but even then, it will not fulfill the narcissist's need. Regardless of how much and how often you tell a narcissist about your love and admiration for them, it will never be enough. A narcissist's psyche is such that he truly believes that he is incapable of being loved by others. In spite of the façade of self-absorption and a sense of grandiose, a narcissist is often insecure and afraid of never being able to measure up. He craves praise and approval from others because it helps to bolster his fragile ego.

Extremely controlling

Narcissists are almost always disappointed with the way life turns out, so they try to do everything they can to control and shape it according to their wishes. They not only need to be controlled, but they demand that they must be in control. Their sense of entitlement and superiority only fuels their belief that they must be in control of everything. Not just that, narcissists will also have a specific storyline in their mind for every character in their life. They expect others to behave and react in the manner they have imagined in their mind. When this doesn't happen—in fact, it seldom does—it just makes narcissists feel unsettled and upset. They are incapable of predicting what will happen next since you are going "off-script." So, don't be surprised if you notice that narcissists will often demand that you must speak and behave in a specific manner so that they can retain their sense of control. You are merely a character in the play that the narcissists are directing. Narcissists fail to see that others are separate entities with their own thoughts and desires.

The unmistakable feeling of superiority

Narcissists tend to live in a two-dimensional world where everything is either black or white. Everyone and everything can be classified as good or bad, right or wrong, and superior or inferior. There exists a specific hierarchy in their minds, and they are obviously present in the top tier. A narcissist will feel safe only when he thinks he is at the top. A narcissist always feels like he must be the absolute best; he must always be right and should be able to control everyone around him. A narcissist also thinks people must always do things the narcissist's way.

It is quite interesting to note that a narcissist can also experience this feeling of superiority by being the absolute worst, or even the most upset. If they feel like this, they tend to think that they are entitled to receive concern or empathy, and they may even think that they have the right to hurt others or demand an apology to make things right. A sense of absolute superiority and entitlement are amongst the defining traits of a narcissist.

Absence of boundaries

Narcissists are incapable of seeing where they end and where you begin. They are quite similar to toddlers. They seem to think that everything belongs to them, that everyone thinks as they do, and that everyone wants the same things they do. In fact, narcissists will be quite shocked and affronted if they realize this isn't true.

If narcissists desire something from you, they will go to great lengths to get what they want. The narcissists can be extremely persistent in their quest for getting what they want from you or others.

Shrugs all responsibility

A narcissist does love to be in control, but he will never want to accept any responsibility for the turn of events unless everything goes the way he planned and the desired results are obtained. When things don't proceed according to his plan or when he receives any criticism, the narcissist will conveniently shift all the responsibility and the blame onto others. It has to be someone else's fault because narcissists are the epitome of perfection, at least, according to themselves. Since they are perfect, if things don't go as planned, it must be someone else's fault. At times, the blame can be quite generalized—the police, the management, the teachers, the government, and so on. At times, the blame can be quite specific. The narcissist might pick a specific individual to blame like his parents, the law, or even the judge. Usually, a narcissist tends to blame the person that he is quite close to.

To enable the fragile façade of perfection, a narcissist will often find someone to blame. If you happen to be the person the narcissist is closest to, then be prepared to take the blame. You will be the safest person to blame because the chances of you leaving the narcissist are quite slim, and this makes him feel safe.

Desire for perfection

Narcissists have a desire for perfection and expect it from everyone and everything around them as well as themselves. They believe that they must be perfect, you must be perfect, and the events in life must be as expected and that their life needs to unfold precisely in the manner they envisioned. This exaggerated need for demanding the impossible is the reason why a narcissist often feels quite miserable and dissatisfied. Their constant need for perfection makes them complain constantly.

Complete lack of empathy

Only when you can understand others and can see where they are coming from will you be able to empathize with them. A narcissist cannot empathize with others. In fact, it is safe to say that narcissists are devoid of all empathy. They are selfish, self-absorbed, and self-centered. These traits prevent a narcissist from ever being able to understand the feelings of others fully. Narcissists seldom give a conscious thought about what others might think or feel; after all, they expect others to think as they do. Also, a narcissist might not experience guilt or remorse and may rarely—if ever—apologize.

That said, narcissists are quite adept at identifying any alleged threats, anger, and rejection from others around him. At the same time, they are quite oblivious to the feelings and emotions of others around them. They often misinterpret simple minute facial expressions and are biased while interpreting the same. Unless you display your emotions dramatically, narcissists are incapable of accurately assuming what you are experiencing. Even saying something as simple as "I love you" or "I am sorry" can backfire easily if the narcissists are in a foul mood. They might not believe you and will assume that your comment was an attack instead.

Apart from this, if your words and expressions are not in sync, the narcissists will respond incorrectly. It is the reason why most narcissists fail to understand sarcasm or jokes and think of them as a personal attack. Their inability to properly read body language is another reason why narcissists aren't empathetic. They cannot perceive emotions correctly, and they tend to misinterpret them. They also don't believe that you can think and act in a manner different from theirs.

Narcissists cannot understand the nature of feelings. They don't understand how feelings manifest. They believe their feelings are often the result of an external force or action. They don't realize that their feelings are a manifestation of their biochemistry, their thoughts, and their perceptions. Simply put, narcissists believe you are responsible for what they feel, especially all the negative ones.

They come to this conclusion because you deviated from their plan or because you made them feel insecure. So, the only logical recourse in a narcissist's mind is to blame you. This apparent lack of empathy certainly makes it quite difficult to establish a true and meaningful relationship with a narcissist.

CHAPTER 3: NARCISSIST PERSONALITY DISORDER AND TREATMENT OPTIONS

WHAT CAUSES NPD?

Experiences during childhood are known to be significant towards the development of this disorder. There are genetic markings which contribute and initiate a high vulnerability for the problem, in the same way, there would be for other mental illness types. Without a high genetic predisposition when it comes to narcissism, then NPD is not likely to develop unless there are environmental agents which are uncharacteristically strong and help to initiate such situations. The question of genetics and personality issues, in general, has been thoroughly studied in the recent times for some disorders more than others,but there has been a consistent connection illustrated between narcissistic attributes and factors that can be inherited. The effect is not exactly overwhelming,but it would be strong enough to play a big role in the development of the disorder.

As such, there is estimation that about 6 percent of the American population has a narcissistic personality disorder that happens to be more common in men as well and has roots that begin in childhood. The nature of the way it is oriented as a disorder means the individual is extremely resistant to any treatment. This severe illness leads the individuals to create chaos as they create a lot of harm to others on a sociological level. Before considering how demands for support of ego and desires, there should be an analysis of pertinent normal child development. Small children for one are naturally selfish as a normal part of their development in which they work to have their needs considered and met.

Until this point, they are not able to understand the needs and desires of others and how it relates to their own in the scheme of things. As teens, the kids typically become self-centered as they continue to struggle for self-identity. As opposed to self-centeredness that generally decreases, children should then start to develop healthy and long-lasting esteem to protect and care for others while still caring about themselves. This is to deviate from dangerous influences and to stay connected to the family and the society as a whole. Healthy levels of esteem are indicative that the child believes they are loved and are worthy of their societal level,so they do not deserve to be mistreated or have a thick skin for it. More importantly, they start to get a feel for themselves what it should be like to treat others and what it entails to live adequately within the communal setting. Now, unfortunately,the narcissism that is in particular children will not be detected typically as children are expected to act in a self-centered manner. After all, one might say they are just acting in their own self-interest or that they do not know any better. Considering the discipline levels of the current society, the levels of empathy are steadily falling in children,and so it is getting quite hard to tell which an issue with morality is and what a danger sign is for a future narcissist.

The typical childhood self-centeredness has to change to pave the way for mental stability when the child starts to become an adult. To grow up able to function in the right way in families, the kids have to gradually gain the stability to see the perspectives of others and empathy as concerns the suffering of other people. Healthy children should then show a gradual development in this sector and show sincere signs of caring about the wellbeing of others. Now developing a sense of empathy while a child is growing up is a big warning sign of a serious personality issue as an adult and is one of the warning signs for narcissism in the adult stages. The question though is whether the children that develop into narcissists and showed the warning signs of morality and empathy early on were born with it or the environment was a factor early on from the time they were born.

In 2008 there was a study carried out in Scandinavia which considered 3000 nonidentical twins and genetic factors were found to have a 25 percent influence on the development of narcissistic traits in the participants of the study. Environmental influences covered the remaining percentage of course. There was another study that was done in Asia recently on two particular attributes for NPD which was a sense of entitlement and feelings of being grandiose. The study showed there was an inheritance factor of 23 percent for feelings of grandiosity and 35 percent for entitlement. That means the children had a 35 chance of having entitlement and a lower chance of having feelings of grandiosity which is the stronger narcissistic trait. This confirms the contributions of genetic effects even when the narcissistic symptoms are analyzed when in isolation.

There was another study done by Lindsey in 2007 where narcissism, as measured by a standardized test, became a common inherited trait. In the study,175 volunteer twin pairs were gotten from the general population. Each of them did a questionnaire which was an assessment of eighteen characteristics of a personality disorder. The authors estimated the heritability for each of the characteristics through standard methodology then giving estimates concerning the relative contribution of genetic causation. Narcissism, in this case, was found to have the highest level of heritability, and this means the trait is the identical twins was influenced a lot by genetics. When it came to the other seventeen attributes, only four of them were found to be statistically significant such as identity problems, contrarianism, and callousness.

Similarly, advances made in technology such as brain imaging has proven that the brains of the ones suffering from issues like NPD, BPD,and Antisocial Personality Disorder which happen to be in the same cluster are not exactly functioning in the right manner. The activity levels when it comes to the brains of those suffering from the condition are said to be abnormal. Research done on cluster B type of personality disorders has also confirmed a lot of physiological brain dysfunction in two of the four cluster B problems. The reason why the brain is not functioning as it should is not yet known though. There is not a lot of research which has been done regarding this approach on NPD because most narcissists do not usually admit to having any problems unless they are forced to do so by their families or by the society. In fact, you might find that most available narcissists are those who are incarcerated for crimes done due to their condition. Additional research on conditions within the same spectrum has shown that these personality disorders have a rate of appearance in offspring at 68%. That would mean two-thirds of the children of the people that have issues with narcissism may also have it themselves. Overall the fact that brain imaging shows that people with this cluster B issues are quite different from the images of normal brain patterns shows that genetics does have a stake in the development of narcissistic personality disorder. These brain function patterns would not be influenced by environmental factors to become a certain way unless, through hard trauma, drugs or disease but these are farfetched reasons. This is not to say that environmental causes do not have a stake in creating narcissistic personality issues, but the genetics lay the foundation for these types of individuals. The brain functions of NPD patients are already wired in a certain way. It is the environmental factors which then capitalize on the already sowed potential to bring out these types of people in the society.

THE DIAGNOSTIC CRITERIA FOR NPD

There is a narcissistic personality inventory (NPI) tool based on forced choice questions meant for measuring narcissism in populations of people and a diagnostic tool called the Millon Clinical Multiaxial Inventory (MCMI) used more for individual cases that can be and often are used by medical professionals to diagnose NPD (narcissist personality disorder). These tools can be helpful but they cannot be used by themselves. They must be used in conjunction with observations of patient behavior. In order to be diagnosed and get treatment for NPD, a patient's condition should meet the criteria for a diagnosis of NPD as defined in the Diagnostic and Statistical Manual of Mental Disorders (DSM-5).

NPD Behavioral Characteristics

The manifestations of narcissist personality disorder are an extreme (some even call it erotic) self-interest that often involves an emphasis on physical appearance. If one is diagnosed with narcissism personality disorder (NPD), it will generally result as a consequence of a psychiatrist or other qualified health professional observing the patient behaving as if he or she is without the capacity to love anyone but themselves. Most of the time they are unable to provide their significant other, friends and other family members with the love, friendship and caring they all need for a healthy two-way relationship.

Also, the patient exhibits a behavior totally lacking in empathy, disregarding other people's feelings and ignoring what others in their life care about. They have never "felt anyone else's pain" or even tried to empathize with someone going through a difficult time. In fact, there is only one perspective on the world that exists to the narcissist: their own.

With NPD the narcissist will often have an unrealistic and "out of touch with reality" overconfidence and vanity. They will view their appearance and capabilities as far better than they actually are yet they are unable to deal with even the slightest of criticism. They will hunger for and even demand praise and admiration from those in their life.

Other People Live To Meet The Needs Of The Narcissist

Relating to the early paper by Martin Buber referred to earlier in this book, Buber recognized that narcissists view other people as objects to be used for achieving their ends rather than treating people as equal human beings. They will use others to achieve their own ends without the slightest thought of what it may cost the other person.

A Lack Of Appropriate Boundaries

This "people are objects to be used" attitude can create a very strange situation whereby the narcissist cannot distinguish between himself or herself and others. So the narcissistic views others as an extension of themselves and thinks that others exist only to meet their needs. If it turns out that the other people in their life do not exist for this purpose then the narcissist doesn't even recognize their existence.

That's right! Other people don't even exist in the mind of the narcissist if they are not living to meet the every need of the narcissist. This is called the lack of the ability to recognize boundaries. In other words, other people are extensions of themselves and are expected to behave the way the narcissist expects them to and live up to each and every one of their expectations. There is no boundary between the narcissist and others. For those that the narcissists view as true extensions of themselves, they heap on unwarranted flattery and admiration so as to maintain the affirmation of their unrealistic and inflated self worth.

Oblivious

Another behavior of the narcissist is a lack of awareness and insight. They have no idea they have a mental illness and are totally unaware of the impact their behavior has on others. This can make it very difficult to treat narcissists. This also makes it nearly impossible for them to have normal relationships with other people. All of their interaction with the other people in their lives is focused on themselves making the continuation of any kind of favorable two-way relation that they start extremely difficult for the other person.

Lack of Appropriate Emotion

The narcissist does not have the ability to feel appropriate relational emotions because their life is not about others...it's only about them. So not only do they not have normal love emotions, they also either repress totally or never really feel emotions like regret when they should. After hurting someone else emotionally, even committing acts of violence, when they should feel shame and remorse they do not. They live a life never apologizing, asking for forgiveness or for that matter even feeling bad about hurting other people emotionally or physically.

Conversely, when someone does something for them that is extraordinary and a person would normally feel the emotion of gratitude and thank them appropriately, the narcissist will not express gratitude. This is because everyone in the narcissist's life is expected to do wonderful things for the narcissist and it's not "normal" when they don't. In fact, as we will explore next, the emotion that is most likely felt when there is a lack of pandering and admiring the narcissist is called injury and rage.

CHAPTER 4: THE ACTIONS AND THOUGHTS OF A NARCISSIST

Trying to get into a narcissist's mind is hard to do. Everyone acts and thinks differently and each person is unique in the way they react and approach situations. A narcissist has a set behavioral pattern and this makes them stand out. While there might be some anomalies in places, since everybody is different, there are two examples:

- <u>Using Covert or Overt Methods</u>

For a narcissist to manipulate a situation or person so their needs are met, they might use methods that are described as either overt or covert. Overt is very obvious, where covert methods are very secret and slide under the radar. Covert methods are very destructive to others and this is why people who are in a relationship with a narcissist have problems leaving. They begin to questions whether it is them or me. A classic method is gaslighting.

A normal narcissist will always use overt methods. A vulnerable narcissist is going to use covert methods. Malignant or toxic narcissist are going to use a mixture of both.

- Cerebral or Somatic Approach

This is talking about the way a narcissist appreciated themselves and things. A narcissist who uses somatic methods will be totally taken by how they look, their general appearance, and their body. They are extremely vain. The cerebral method is using their brain, and seeming to be very intelligent. This narcissist will take great lengths to convince others that their opinion is needed and the only one that matters.

It is important to identify the type of narcissist that you are dealing with. While it could be hard to pinpoint exactly, you should be able to identify the dangerous type. A malignant or toxic narcissist won't have any problem hurting other people and won't show any remorse. This narcissist damages everybody around them. Anybody who is lucky enough to get out of a relationship with this type of narcissist is going to need a lot of emotional support or therapy after.

You may be reading this and wondering how anybody can't see there are things wrong with how they are thinking and acting. This is exactly how NPD works. You have to remember that narcissism is a personality disorder and this creates a warped way of thinking. Narcissists will completely 100 percent think that you are wrong, and you should see their uniqueness. You shouldn't argue with them since they are always right. They will never look at themselves and think that they might be wrong. They might think that they would have handled the situation differently and better. True narcissists don't wee a problem with how they act or think. When dealing with malignant or toxic narcissist, these people don't see a problem with hurting others for their own gain.

Why Narcissist Won't Get Treated

Many narcissists won't realize that there is a problem. If somebody tells them they should seek help since they are showing narcissistic behaviors, they will laugh or turn it around on you.

This isn't true for everybody. If a person has a mild form of narcissism, there could be an "aha" moment where they might think: "hey, I wonder if this applies to me", when they are reading about narcissism or if somebody points out they are showing narcissistic behaviors. This is extremely rare and unlikely that a vulnerable or classic narcissist will ever seek help.

Will they get help? With some, they will but only after they have self-destructed or hurt someone close to them very badly. If a moment pushes them to a point, it might be medical help might be accepted. In spite of all that, it is still unlikely and it is a very sad fact.

Will Treatment Help?

There are various treatments for narcissism, but many center around challenging thought patterns and behavioral changes. In extreme cases, it might be recommended that they be hospitalized, especially for extreme narcissists who have become very self-destructive.

The biggest problem is that treatment centers around solving the incident instead of solving the condition.

Can treatment help? It could, if they seek help, but it will take a lot of commitment and effort on the narcissist's part. Treatment isn't easy, and this goes for any type of problem that requires challenging thoughts and mindsets along with cognitive behavioral therapy. This treatment method won't be successful overnight and is going to require a long time along with maintenance treatment after that.

Personality Disorders Like Narcissism

Many mental health problems and personality disorders are linked together in some ways. A person that suffers from depression could also have anxiety. A person who has stress could also suffer from anxiety. A person who has been diagnosed with bipolar disorder might have narcissistic behaviors. A person who has been diagnosed with a borderline personality disorder might have NPD, too.

In spite of all of that, there are three personality disorder that link closely to NPD:

- Histrionic personality disorder

- Antisocial personality disorder

- <u>Borderline personality disorder</u>

A healthcare professional can assess if a certain type of disorder is there but talking someone into seeking help is hard especially if they have narcissism.

Dealing with the Abuser

Now that you have decided to cut ties with your narcissist, you might be wondering if it is fine to remain friends with this person? In specific cases, it could be impossible to totally shut the door on your abuser even if you want to. Immediate family, friends, and coworkers you have to constantly see will have a presence in your life.

Can you still be nice to them? The answer is no and yes. First, nobody expects you to "clean things up" with your abuser. If you feel that remaining civil would work best, them it could work out. While we are on the topic of being civil, is it possible to be civil to a narcissist. It is questionable if they can understand or adapt to that.

Resuming a relationship after a fight with a narcissist will take repentance and an apology from the offender, and, remember that a narcissist won't ever take the blame for anything, even if you know they did it. Without apologizing, the narcissist won't even think about being civil.

What does this mean for you? Simply that trying to have a "civil" relationship may be one sided. Unfortunately, your abuser might take this opportunity to embarrass you if you try to initiate contact.

You could try to reach out and talk about the upcoming family reunion, but they might totally ignore or dismiss you once you begin talking. This is something they might do if there are other people around that see they are treating you with hatred.

Seeing as the narcissist has a pristine image with the other people who are around you, the people that see you being treated negatively will take the narcissist's side, that is if you did something wrong.

In many cases, the best thing to do after breaking up with a narcissist is to completely avoid them. Ignoring and treating them like a non-entity could be more beneficial for your emotional and mental healing. This will keep you from being drawn back into their trap. It also makes sure your abuse won't be able to exploit you.

Is it going to be easy? No, most narcissistic abuse victims say the urge to reach out and talk or to ask forgiveness could pop up at any moment while you are healing from the abuse. This might even happen years after you have left the relationship.

Even though it may be hard, it isn't impossible. Try the following strategies to help you heal and strengthen your resolve to keep your distance from the abuser:

- Get Rid of All Communication

Block. Unfriend. Unfollow. This may sound harsh but in this digital age, it is the worst thing you could do to somebody who is on social media. You also have to cut all ties that you have or they could try to reach you in other ways to try and rekindle the flame.

What if I really have to speak with them? Don't allow this thought to drive you to open ways of communication. What is important right now is you. You have to keep your focus on recovering. Make sure not to leave any windows or doors open and don't allow any opportunities to let your internal mechanism push you into a conversation.

- Don't Update Your Life on Social Media

Nowadays, it's easy to find information on anybody's current activities and preoccupations. They don't call it the internet superhighway for no reason. Bad news is this could make it easier to keep checking on your abuser by getting tidbits of information on their life.

The biggest problem with stalking them online is it could spark flames. One flame is longing: the more you look at their updates and photos, the more you want to be back into their lives. The other flame is sadness: you see their life is going on without you, and even though they aren't affected by your absence could injure your self-worth.

You need to remember that narcissists are masters of disguise. They are great at pretending. Your absence might have caused them some distress, they will make sure not to show you this. They are expecting you to look at their life. They have made sure to have images ready to hit you with.

- Think about the Truth

Even if you know you are right, you have a tendency to give other people the benefit of the doubt. This is just how reasonable people are. Even if you are dealing with an abuser, victims need to look at other angles. They might be hurting as well. They might have low self-esteem. They might be troubled.

Nobody other than you deserves your kindness and compassion. Narcissists aren't troubled people. They don't want to be fixed. They aren't acting out of trauma. This is the problem with narcissism. They don't "deserve" compassion that most of us give to others.

Narcissists think they are better than others because they were brought up to believe they are. They fight to control everybody in their lives since they feel like they are entitled to power. They often think: "I am better than you, therefore you should listen to me so you can somehow achieve the same greatness." It is a complete toxic mentality.

Don't try to make sense of why they are acting the way they do. Try to think about the truth behind the actions. Yes, it is going to hurt at the beginning to see the behavior for what it really is, but make your mind see the truth and it will be easier to keep your distance when they lose their luster and take on their true form in your mind.

- Stay Preoccupied

There isn't any strategy that is more effective that just keeping your abuser out of your mind. Your focus needs to be on you so do things that show yourself that you love yourself. When you constantly think about the painful abuse, it can be very negative if done to excess.

Take yourself out on a date, find a new hobby, and buy yourself something new. It will be better if you can find something you enjoy without needing anyone else's company. The more you can show yourself love, the faster you will find your self-worth. When that is in place, it will be easier to see the abuser for what they really are. This lets you detach yourself from your abuser further.

CHAPTER 5: CAN TREATMENT BE SUCCESSFUL?

Since narcissism is classified as a personality disorder, those in the psychological community have created tools and methods to allow the narcissist to better cope with their abnormal emotions and behaviors. However, no magic pill can simply stop someone from being a narcissist.

It can also be hard to treat a narcissist because it is not easy for them to admit they are wrong and need help. They can view someone recommending they get help as a betrayal. A psychologist or psychiatrist can also be perceived as a threat to their distorted fantasy life and sense of superiority.

Should a narcissist agree to seek treatment, psychotherapy is generally where it starts. This involves different forms of talk therapy, including individual and group. This works to aid the person in working toward healthier relationships because they can learn to better relate to others. Over time and with regular therapy, they may be able to find relationships more enjoyable, intimate and rewarding. This therapy can also help them understand the root of their emotions and what is driving them to distrust others, compete or despise others.

The areas of change that therapy targets are directed at helping a person to accept responsibility and learn to:

- Maintain and accept collaboration with coworkers and personal relationships

- Regulate feelings and understand them

- Alleviate the desire for conditions and goals that are unattainable

- Accept what they can accomplish and maintain

- Discover and cope with any specific issues associated with their low self-esteem

- Accept and recognize their own potential and competence

- Learn to tolerate criticism

For the most part, psychotherapy is what is recommended. However, there are instances where professionals might recommend medications. For example, if the person is experiencing anxiety or depression, medications to aid in controlling these might be tried.

Outside of the therapy sessions, the professional might suggest certain tools and methods a person can use to complement their sessions. Keeping an open mind is highly stressed. The narcissist should focus on the rewards that treatment can help to provide them. It is imperative to realize that setbacks can happen. By focusing on the potential rewards, this may help the person to stay on track with treatment.

Keeping up with treatment is also important. This means that any medications should be taken exactly as directed and all therapy sessions should be attended. This all contributes to the narcissist being able to remain focused on their goal. A professional may set up series of small goals that they will help the person to work toward. As they accomplish each of the mini goals, it can help them to see that progress is being made, so should a setback occur, they can see that they are still doing better than they were before.

If the person has any other mental health conditions, or a problem with substance abuse, treatment for these should be tackled. A healthcare professional can help them to determine which additional treatments might be needed and beneficial.

CHAPTER 6: OTHER PERSONALITY DISORDERS RELATED TO NARCISSISM

There are many indicators used to identify a narcissist, but this is not to say that everyone displaying these behaviors is suffering from narcissism. Remember narcissism is a psychological disorder and as so, other psychological disorders may manifest through the same characteristics as those displayed by a narcissist. The characteristics we shall look at can give you further insight into the mind of a narcissist, which can be very helpful when you are dealing with someone suffering from the condition.

Fear of Rejection

A narcissist is usually suffering from an emotional trauma. He harbors fears of rejection. In fact, more than anything else, this is the one thing he fears the most in the world. He or she is highly attuned to anything that he (for all intents and purpose, he should be taken to mean the narcissist person) considers signs of impending rejection. He believes that rejection is a shameful thing that is an experience only for the weak. He builds a wall around him and does not let anyone close. He believes that he can be rejected or disappointed only if he piles up too much hope on someone. He tends to value material things like wealth more than relationships and will literally be more in love with material things than actual people. He will cheat, manipulate, and lie to protect himself and keep people from glimpsing the weak person he knows himself to be. He builds up a façade and makes himself accept it as a reality, refusing to see the real world without his filter. With a self-proclaimed sense of importance he fails to see the logic behind why a person like him would ever have to hear a "no". If he was brought up as a spoilt brat he is used to having his way all the time and goes into depression and anxiety when something doesn't go his way.

Have a False Self

We have already seen that a child raised in what society considers a normal, healthy home setting develops into his true self. A child brought up in an unhealthy home on the other hand, does not get this chance. He spent his entire childhood trying to grow into someone else's shoes that he did not bother finding his own. Be it an over achiever kid constantly trying to impress his parents or a rowdy teenager who goes out of his way to disappoint his family, every potential narcissist develops a false identity or self. At times they may also become mildly schizophrenic which may fully develop into multiple personalities later on. He thinks that the only person who is truly capable of appreciating him is himself. It shouldn't be surprising if he discusses most of his problems with his other self or imaginary friend. In this way, he also justifies having looked at a problem from different angles. Therefore, he grows up without knowing who he truly is. He develops a false self and because he is in a desperate search for what he thinks is the ideal love, he is unable to connect intimately with anyone. Love and affection may hit him right in the face but he may not realize it because he is constantly in search of the extraordinary. This is mainly because of his fear for betrayal, rejection, and abandonment. He does not let anyone get too close to him and maintains a distance from everyone.

Additionally, because he does not really know himself and hides behind his false self, it is impossible for anyone to get close enough to form a substantive relationship with him. People who do get close enough are hurt and sent off in such a way that they wouldn't even consider rekindling the relationship again. Moreover, because of his entitlement, he is capable of one selfless act "any act directed at himself" which is not unlike the Greek mythology of Narcissus.

Have a Narcissistic Circle

Due to his desire to be around people who he thinks worship or admire him, he will have a circle. Imagine the most popular kid in high school. He is likely to have his own band of followers who hang out with him all the time. Either out of respect or to prevent themselves from being picked on. The narcissistic circle is somewhat similar. This circle consists of people who constantly remind the narcissist that he is the greatest thing that happened to the world. They add fuel to his already burning ego-fire. This circle comprises of people who are termed as Narcissist supply.

Narcissist supply is a group of people who provide the narcissist with the approval, attention and admiration he craves. The false self in the narcissist needs this supply source and he deems it necessary for his survival. Because of this constant barrage of admiration, either false or otherwise, the narcissist's ego inflates like an air balloon. He depends on this steady stream of admiration and attention to feed his ego. Unknown to himself, he begins to depend on this circle more than he would like to admit. When looking at the big picture it reminds us of the bully and his band of cowards who simply use the bigger kid for protection and in return laugh at any joke he makes.

The narcissistic supply circle is no better than the narcissist himself, and because the narcissist is determined to get to the top of his position to get recognition, the supply circle will use the narcissist need for attention to advance their own agenda; be it a promotion at work or special treatment. In most cases, the narcissist is too obsessed with himself to realize that he is being played until it is too late. The circle may have people who might be clever but not as popular or well known as the narcissist. So they cunningly make use of his talents to fuel their own agenda while pacifying the narcissist simultaneously. He sincerely believes that the narcissistic circle simply exists to praise and goad his achievements.

On the other hand, the narcissist is quick to point out to himself that he does not need anyone and the only reason people admire him and offer his praise is because they really feel that way about him. It does not cross his mind that those people might have an ulterior motive and may not be doing the whole thing out of admiration. The narcissist decides that he has to be the center of attention for his supply circle and will not tolerate independence from anyone in the circle. He is firmly rooted in the belief that the circle is there to serve him. Any signs of noncompliance with the needs of the narcissist from anyone in the circle will send him into a rage. He can be quick to anger and his temper is not worth invoking because beyond that line he completely ceases to see all logic and will not calm down until he has had his revenge.

Rage

The narcissist is a very angry person. He uses this rage to scream for the attention he craves. He will scream at anyone in the office because of mundane things. When his narcissistic false self is injured, prepare to see a side of him that is mostly well veiled. When what he considers a narcissistic injury (a threat to his well-cultivated false self, self-esteem and worth) occurs, his rage comes spewing out like an angry volcano. While the rage is raging on, the narcissist is contemplating only one thing, revenge.

To a person who thinks he is always right, a narcissist has an ego that cannot be satiated. So when someone puts him or his actions in the wrong he retaliates in the most violent matter. Rage can also be a publicity stunt for him, where he screams his head off just so that a couple of people turn around and acknowledge that he is a big shot. It is very important to differentiate between anger and narcissistic rage.

Traditional anger triggers or situations that demand for the emotional response of anger do not provoke narcissistic rage. Normal anger is usually incited when someone hurts us or our loved ones or when we see an open act of injustice on an oppressed individual. Normal anger although a bad trait is selfless in its own way. A person is able to see beyond his own problems and stand up for others. A narcissist's rage is his way of scarring people, and when he sees fear on their faces, to him, it is a signal that he has won. This fear fuels their sadistic nature and cements their feelings of importance. It makes no difference to a narcissist that the people around him are getting hurt or unjustly treated. In fact, he might even turn a blind eye on such incidents. His rage is completely invoked only when his physical or emotional self has been hurt. He might go to unreasonable fits of rage if so much as a fingernail on his person is broken but remains completely indifferent if someone is being beaten to death. Due to this rage, the narcissist has no friends or anyone that you and I (normal folks) would call a close friend. In his delusional state, a narcissist thinks that the rage is his way of gaining back his control. His open display of unreasonable rage is his way of exercising control on his personal space and domain.

Need For Control and power

The life of a narcissist has one major driver, domination. He is basically a control freak who would willingly exercise control over the air we breathe if it were up to him. As a person who has problems with rejection, he tries to influence anything and everything around him. When asked for advice, he provides it willingly and follows up on it. He will make sure the person follows his advice to the letter and will not allow him to deviate from his suggestion. When asked for an opinion or small suggestion he expects the person to dissolve any other ideas he might have had and religiously follow the one that the narcissist provided. A narcissist lives to dominate everything he touches; his workplace, every person he interacts with, and social events. He does not look at power as "power with" but looks at it as "power over". He uses power and control as his springboard for emotional and verbal abuse. He enjoys being able to look down on people and stepping on them from time to time. Although narcissists have good control over power from a practical point of view, that level of control is not something the other people would look forward to. When in the driver's seat, the narcissist would be the only one enjoying the ride. He has opinions on the correct way of doing things, either at home or at work. However, when it comes to the actual implementation of the plan, he has no desire to be hands on. He believes he is too precious for menial work. So although he has opinions on every small detail, he will not be bothered to burn calories over any of it. He firmly decides that the whole thing will go smoothly only if he is placed in the manager's chair. His idea of control would be to constantly nag people about not doing their work properly. When one of his colleagues does finish their work on time and in a very good way, he gives them credit for it half-heartedly.

For example, in a home situation, he is very financially restrictive, which leaves him to control the entire expenditure. He thinks that every basic need of the family has to pass through him and wants people to ask him for permission before they do anything. He is extremely happy when people ask him for permission to do something. In fact, he thinks it is downright outrageous that people would leave him out of the loop. He is quick to condemn anyone he thinks is not doing something the correct way, his way. He reluctantly gives credit when deserved, and complains through the whole process idea. In his delusion, he believes that ultimately, he deserves all the praise because to him, the success of the plan is because of him. His ideology entitles him to the full credit behind the success of any plan he was involved in, even if his contribution was close to nothing. On the other hand, if the plan fails, it is the fault of junior officers and not him. Just as good as he is at taking credit for things he didn't do, he is equally agile at throwing the blame on others for something that might have been entirely his fault.

Seeks Grandiosity

This is the most outstanding and most discriminating feature of any narcissist. His perspective at life shows him in an awesome light and the others on a level beneath him. A narcissist convinces himself that he is one of the most important people on the planet. He believes that the events that led up to his life since his birth has some grand reason or phenomenal divine planning behind it. He has an unrealistic overvaluation of his abilities and talents. Regardless of how talented he might be, a narcissist always tends to over sell himself by exaggerating his abilities. The superiority complex kicks in and he decides that all his abilities and skills are the best that anyone can get. He is preoccupied with himself, fantasies of power, success, beauty, and believes that he is superior and unique. Due to this, he is boastful, self-centered, pretentious, and self-referential. He lives a lot in dreams, where he glorifies his existence in such a grand manner that he has to build up a façade of grandiosity just to make his reality worth living.

In the archives of general psychiatry, the narcissist exaggerates his abilities, achievements, talents, and capacity to cover his lack thereof. Admitting that he lacks certain skill sets that a rival or fellow worker might have hurts his ego so he exaggerates to a very dangerous level. Sky is the limit for such self-wound fantasies. He believes that he has no limitations and due to his grandiose fantasies, he believes that he does not need anyone.

Cannot Handle Shame

To the narcissist, there is a fine line between his perfectionism and grandiosity. He feels inadequate when he fails to get something he wants. Rejection, lack of control over his surroundings and a lack of attention may also bring about this sense of uselessness. Coincidentally, when the narcissist experiences shame, he feels inferior and full of flaws. This causes injuries to his narcissistic false self. In spite of all the grand build up, there are times when a narcissist has to accept reality. In most cases, this reality is accompanied by shame and an inferiority complex. This stark contrast to his perfect fantasy world is a huge emotional blow to the narcissist. He becomes extremely volatile and unpredictable. At this stage, he is in a complete rage directing the anger at anyone in his vicinity. He feels inadequate, exposed, and vulnerable and this overwhelms him. So to vent out this negative energy, he turns viciously onto the people in his immediate vicinity. The reason or logic behind the rage may or may not be justified. As far as he is concerned, he tries to call away the attention from his inferior self by indulging in mindless acts of violence.

Seeks Perfectionism

A narcissist is obsessive, and the false self governs his obsession. This obsession over perfection and method entitle him to produce better quality work than his peers. He sets unachievable and downright impossible goals to achieve. Due to his unrealistic goals and grandiosity, he is always struggling to reach and accomplish goals and feels a lot of shame when he cannot. The tasks that he set for himself may be beyond normal human capacity but he cannot process failure as something that might have happened to anybody. He pressurizes himself into believing that even the most fouled plan will work if he is in charge of it because of his superiority and uniqueness. He also believes that even if other people are able to pull it off, they can never do it with his mind blowing level of perfection.

Additionally, because the narcissist thinks in the lines of "all right or all wrong" (no middle ground) or all "white and black", all his achievements have to be either of the one ways. He does not believe in a compromise. All his results and achievements have to be a soaring success or it is deemed as a failure. Accomplishments that fall short of his grandiosity are complete failures in his sights, and because he thinks he knows everything there is to know in his field of study, he has no room for learning. He will not accept that he has room for improvement, as he is already perfect in every aspect. Every project he undertakes has to be a "eureka" moment or to him, it is a complete failure. He might be able to take a project to a sixty percent success but he will not consider that an achievement, he will drop the entire idea and start on something else in search of that one path breaking moment. When that moment happens, he is extremely elated and boastful about it that he will speak about it for years. This "eureka" moment stokes his ego.

When he does not achieve his goals, his sense of perfectionism and uniqueness feels compromised. He feels devalued, shameful, and vulnerable. Failure enrages him and fills him with self-loath and doubt. He will reprimand himself, which in turn will stroke his rage. When he falls short of his perfectionist tendencies, he experiences a great deal of shame as an ongoing tug of war between balancing grandiosity and perfectionism. Each failure makes him more unstable than he already is. So if a narcissist has been failing continuously or quite some time then his chances of losing his sanity are very high.

Frequently Bored

The narcissist is in a constant never-ending search for excitement in his life. He uses the excitement to feel good about himself. A narcissist is an adrenaline junkie. They will definitely jump off the plane or do a bungee jump; they will chase all kinds of thrills in the hope that it will cement their uniqueness and help ease the rage they may always have. He is in a never ending search for new thrills. No hobby can hold him down as it is only a matter of time before he gets bored of it.

They are extremely aggressive and when faced with boredom, the narcissist will plummet into despair. He will do everything to avoid this despair because it brings with it those feelings of helplessness, despair, and a need for love and admiration. When faced with absolutely nothing to do and no one to turn to, he may also begin actively indulging in degrading addictive practices. He is always willing to explore something new just to rid himself of boredom. Whether the practice in question has a negative effect on him is only secondary as his primary objective is to keep himself busy. From a third person's point of view it does make sense to keep a narcissist occupied; preferably with some harmless activity to keep him off the streets. His uncontrolled flow of emotion is most likely to endanger himself and others around him.

To the narcissistic person, boredom creates anxiety and siphons out every bit of their morale. For this very reason, the narcissist will not tolerate boredom for long. If their narcissistic supply chain is not available, you will find the narcissist performing activities that attract a lot of attention to him. Just as much as he craves to be the center of attention, he is sufficiently equipped to grab the attention for himself.

Constantly Seeking Fame

The narcissist is always looking for glory. He will do anything to be in the limelight because to him, being in the limelight is proof of acceptance and admiration from his peers. All this is in the hope that the fame and subsequent admiration will help fill the emptiness from childhood that cannot go away.

The constant need for admiration is because of the intolerable need for human contact he lacked as a child or the sense of entitlement he developed as a child. Due to the constant struggle between his true and false self, the narcissist will suffer from multiple personality disorder. When he is feeling shame, out of control, or inadequate, he will split off to the personality that he feels safe in.

A point to note here is that while the narcissist will experience shame, the shame is not specifically directed at himself, rather outwards, towards other people rather than the self. This is so that he can preserve the self from taking responsibility or experiencing any backlash such as unworthiness or self-contempt. To elevate these feelings when they creep up, the narcissist will retreat to his narcissistic supply or place themselves in a situation they are bound to receive a lot of praise for whatever reason. The fame makes him feel alive, wanted, and desired.

The more desired he feels, the more grandiose he gets, and the more arrogant he gets. While he is being celebrated, he takes this to be an affirmation of his importance, or rather, the importance of his fake self. He gets overly confident and verbose and he will go to great lengths to display his newly found celebrity status. At this stage of his self-assuredness and self-confidence, the narcissist operated at the illusion that crossing him in the wrong way will lead to retribution.

CHAPTER 7: COMMON NARCISSISTIC SITUATIONS YOU MAY ENCOUNTER

Since anyone can suffer from narcissistic personality disorder, this means that you might be working with or for one, have a partner with narcissistic tendencies or even a family member or friend. So here are ways to help you deal with these people.

FRIENDSHIP SITUATIONS

There is one person in your social circle that might be suffering from narcissistic personality disorder. A narcissistic friend is someone who always loves to go out and talk all day or night about his or her life without even bothering to ask how you have been. However, casting a narcissist friend away is not a great way to deal with them.

- When your narcissist friend asks you for a favor, step back a little and see what his or her goals are. Your friend's favors might be innocent but they might be using them to gauge whether you will easily fall in her trap or not.
- Treat you friend as neutral as you can. Don't show them that you favor them over your other friends because this will give your friend a sign that you can easily be manipulated.

- Don't divulge anything about yourself that your friend can use against you. Remember that narcissist friends are those who can easily manipulate others if opportunities present themselves. By guarding your personal space, a narcissist friend will not be able to use you easily. This also gives him or her warning that you are setting boundaries in your friendship.

There are times that having a narcissistic friend can be a delight but their overly demanding nature for attention can be very difficult to bear with. These tips will help you effectively deal with a narcissist friend without suffering from any stress.

FAMILY SITUATIONS

While you can opt to stay away from friends or co-workers who have narcissistic personality disorder, staying away from a family member who is suffering from this condition is downright impossible. The thing is that there is no divorcing or firing to solve your problem with a pathologically narcissistic family member. So if you have a mother, father, siblings or an uncle who suffer from this condition, then below are tips on how to deal with them.

- Seek medical help for people who are suffering from narcissistic personality disorder. To get yourself involved with the recovery of your narcissistic relative, you can opt for group therapy. This will help a narcissist family member to understand his or her condition.

- If you have an aunt or uncle who is suffering from narcissistic personality disorder, you can help with the right upbringing of their children by giving them the right environment so that they will grow up without being influenced by their narcissistic parents.

Narcissists, just like other people suffering from personality disorders, are very hard to crack. The best way to deal with these patients is to align with their positive attributes as well as focus on those that they agree are not working. So accept them for who they are but never entertain an illusion that they are capable of emotionally connecting with you.

RELATIONSHIP SITUATIONS

While narcissists can hold on relationships, all of them are not capable into deep commitments. To make matters worse, it is very easy to fall in love with a narcissist given that they have charm and allure. It is important to take note that most narcissists remain faithful during the early stages of relationship because they want their partners to feel secure so that they will worship them throughout the relationship. Eventually, they will show their true nature to their partners. If you are involved in a relationship with a pathological narcissist, here are the things that you need to do:

- Stand your ground and don't let your narcissist partner lead your relationship to any path that he or she wishes to take.

- Insist on counseling for both of you and your partner. However, your narcissist partner may end up resisting the treatment because they won't accept that something is wrong with their personality.

- If all things do not work, your last option is to leave the relationship. Take note that a narcissistic partner will never see you as his or her equal.

Being in a relationship with a partner who is suffering from narcissistic personality disorder can put a strain on the entire relationship despite of your resolve to save it. What you need to do is to guard your heart and seek treatment to help them manage their condition.

AT WORK SITUATIONS

In the study conducted by Zogby International in 2007, the survey firm noted that 37% of employees work for narcissistic bosses. This is a very serious epidemic that needs to be addressed properly. If you are one of the many people who are stuck working with a narcissistic boss or co-worker, below are the things that you can do to deal with them:

- Pitch your new ideas to your boss or co-workers in a group setting. Remember that pathological narcissists have tendencies to steal ideas in order to improve their reputation. By sharing your ideas with the group, you protect yourself and your ideas from being stolen.

- If your boss or coworker blames you for problems that are actually their fault, do not go into blame contagion by blaming other co-workers. What you can do is to trace the cause of the problem to prove your innocence.
- Never stand for being bullied by a narcissistic boss or coworker. If your co-workers have been the witness to the incident, you can ask them to back you up. Never retaliate unless you have proof that you were wronged.
- When working with a narcissist on a project, always assert yourself if you have something to contribute. Never let a narcissistic co-worker decide on everything otherwise the project will fail. Remember that narcissists are great in planning but never in execution. It will help you if you keep track of the contributions of a narcissistic co-worker to prevent them from shirking from their responsibilities.

Dealing with a narcissistic employer or co-worker is a very tough thing to do and if you are targeted by one, shutting them down usually does not work. To protect yourself, make sure that you rehearse your response so that you will not be eventually destroyed by the narcissist.

CHAPTER 8: HOW TO SURVIVE A NARCISSISTIC RELATIONSHIP

Relationships of all kinds with narcissists follow three stages: Love bombing, devaluing, and discarding. This predictable cycle is followed regardless of the type of relationship is forged with the narcissist; narcissists will repeat this with romantic partners, children, friends, and anyone else in their lives who accept it. Those who do not accept it are either demeaned and attacked or completely disregarded and dismissed. While the three stages are followed, narcissists' behavior changes somewhat depending on the kind of relationship and what is socially acceptable within those relationship's norms.

SIGNS YOU ARE IN A RELATIONSHIP WITH A NARCISSIST

A romantic relationship with a narcissist begins perfectly. It feels like it is out of a storybook about true love, and for a good reason; both the storybook and the narcissist's persona are fictitious. The narcissist works hard to draw in his target, seeking to make the target fall hard and fast for the narcissist. This is accomplished through mirroring and love-bombing.

The narcissistic romantic partner may send flowers and love notes to work every day while constantly texting their target about how beautiful they are and how perfect the two of them are together. The romantic partner may invite their target on dates constantly and will push for the relationship to move at a much quicker pace than is typical, even if the target is uncomfortable with it. The narcissist will be more controlling than the target likes, but the target will justify this as being overly-protective or due to past trauma.

Over time, as the target becomes more attached to the narcissist, the narcissist's mask begins to crumble. First it may crack slightly, but eventually, it disintegrates, leaving the narcissist in all his glory, unmasked and unbearable while you find yourself too in love with the mask to leave its pieces on the floor without trying to salvage it. With the victim firmly attached to the narcissist, the narcissist finds he free to be himself. If he feels slighted in any way, he may lash out at the target, saying things that are hurtful or demeaning, or even yelling and intimidating the target into submission.

When in a narcissistic relationship, it is common to feel lonely, or as if you are unimportant, as the narcissist stops putting your desires first as soon as he feels you are firmly within his grasp. He no longer has to go through the effort of winning you over because you have already found yourself head-over-heels in love thanks to the intensely wonderful honeymoon period. He may move on to other tactics to keep you around, such as demeaning you or gas lighting you. You will be left with self-esteem as wounded as the narcissist's, but unlike the narcissist, yours can heal back into something healthy if given the self-care you need.

At the end of the relationship, the narcissist discards you; he may have moved onto a new source to feed his narcissistic supply, or he may have decided that the effort in maintaining you as useful is no longer worthwhile.

IS THERE A FUTURE FOR A RELATIONSHIP TOUCHED BY NARCISSISM?

We have covered a lot of information about the victim's future but what about the narcissist's future.

It isn't a nice picture if the narcissist won't get help. If they don't, it will be likely that they will just jump from one relationship to the next. If they do find a long-term relationship, their partner won't be really fulfilled and happy. They will more than likely just be putting up with the narcissist.

If during the duration of the narcissist's relationship they had children, the bad news is their children will probably develop narcissist behaviors since they were exposed to it through their growing years. Even though there isn't a definite answer to what causes narcissism, there are suggestions that experiences during childhood has firm links toward developing the disorder during their adolescent or adult years.

Narcissists are known to become bitter with time. This is mainly due to people coming into their lives and then leaving them and they can't figure out why. They will always put the blame onto someone else and will never see they had a role in them leaving. Most narcissistic traits get worse with age as they experience more things through their life.

You can see it is a very bleak picture and this is the sad truth about the narcissist's life. People will only stay around if they are treated nice. If they get treated like crap, they will eventually leave. Some might not get to that point but relationships with narcissists are usually empty and don't have respect and true love.

The biggest price any narcissist will pay for their actions with time will be loneliness and not ever knowing what a meaningful relationship really is. The deepest and most meaningful relationship a narcissist will have will be with them.

Should We Blame Social Elements?

You almost know all there is to know about narcissists and the issues and traits that go with it. We also need to look at another area. Are social elements to blame for the increasing number of narcissists?

True narcissists are very rate but it is a term that we hear more and more. For this reason, narcissistic behaviors are more common now, so we need to find out why? Is it all the social pressures we have to deal with? Is it social media? Is it because we are pressured to own the best, look, the best, and be the best?

It is unfair to put the blame of narcissism at modern society's feet. It does make one wonder if it did have a hand in it. Social media makes us aware of the way other people live and look. The influences of social media tell us that if we want to be the best, we must look our best, and this means we have to use a certain product. We get bombarded with people constantly taking selfies and full body photos and then using filters and photoshop to change their appearance drastically. The majority of what we see just isn't real. Now, do you wonder why we have all these unrealistic expectation of what we should look like, what we should be, and what we need to aim for?

No one is completely sure what causes narcissism, so it is the things we are exposed to in life? Most of the narcissistic cases are thought to come from things we experienced during childhood, but what caused those experiences? What makes someone act a specific way? What makes someone create trauma to another human that can cause them to develop a certain personality disorder? It is hard to figure out, but you have to take into account all the possibilities.

We might not completely understand what causes narcissism, and there is a specific amount of stigma attached to it. If we try to be the best, it will be a constant, fruitless task. We should try to just be ourselves.

When talking about future generations, it is our responsibility to make sure our children are brought up to be happy just being who they are, without have to constantly compete to reach unrealistic goals. If we can do this, we are going to raise a generation of young people who are fulfilled, respectful, and well-mannered. These are great boosts toward avoiding trauma and personality disorders.

CHAPTER 9: THE NARCISSIST AND THE EMPATH

WHEN ITS TIME TO LEAVE

At this point, your partner must be willing to at least try to make some changes in their behavior in order to improve their own mental health and your relationship. If your partner is willing to do some of the work, then your relationship can be saved. But, if you have been engaging in the activities discussed previously in this book and your partner still does not see any problem with their behavior, there isn't much hope for an improvement. Unfortunately, as much as we want to believe that we can change another person, we cannot. You can change the dynamics on your end, which can improve the relationship for you, but in order for your partner to truly overcome their narcissistic traits, they have to put in some effort, too. This chapter will outline some of the things that your partner can do to improve their narcissistic tendencies. These techniques are the last step to turn a narcissist into a loving and attentive partner.

Identify the Maladaptive Behaviors that need to be changed

What types of behaviors does your partner see as maladaptive or problematic? This could come from a list that you make or that your partner understands to be true, or a combination of both. Once your partner acknowledges the inappropriate behaviors, he or she can begin to attack and alter them head-on.

Once you both know and understand the types of behaviors to work on, you can set up the positive and negative reinforcement system. Basically, if your partner does something positive to change their behavior, they should be rewarded somehow, and if they engage in one of the behaviors that you are trying to get rid of, a negative reinforcement (often called punishment) should be used like the "No Contact" principle. It works when, for instance, your partner gets abusive, and you distance yourself away from him or her to protect yourself as well as to cool things over. Your partner will eventually realize his or her mistake and will ask you to talk and deal with the problem. The punishments and rewards should be worked out between you both, and your partner has to be willing to commit to this. Many studies have shown that positive reinforcement works better than negative in the long term, so it makes sense to reward all small behaviors in a great way. If these rewards involve both of you, it could be a great way to strengthen your bond.

Practice Service to Others

People can learn to care for others. They have to choose to put the needs of another person before their own needs. If your narcissistic partner is willing to try this, it will be the first step to a loving partnership.

To do so, your partner should put aside one of their needs and do something for you no matter how simple or small it is. Whether that means running an errand that you usually do, making dinner for you, or taking care of one small thing so you don't have to do it, ask your partner to do something, anything for you. Start with something small, and over time, your partner will develop the ability to do more and more for you.

If your partner is willing to do these things for you, it is a good sign that they are willing to change. Talking about each other's needs and deciding what the boundaries are on both sides of the relationship is important. If your partner is amenable to do things for you, you, yourself, should be ready to do things for them as well, especially with regards to their mental health and stability. As we discussed earlier, you have the right to say no to unreasonable demands, but, in a loving relationship, you have to give as well. But first, it must be must be reasonable.

Your partner can learn that providing a service to others will benefit both of you and your partner can develop joy from seeing you happy, but it takes practice. Service to others is important to develop empathy for another person, which is the next step in the process.

Practice Empathy

Simply defined, empathy is the ability to put you in another person's place. By imagining how another person feels, you can relate to them better. The narcissist needs to be able to do this, and it is a skill that takes practice. You can facilitate this by explaining to your partner how you feel when they do a certain thing. As they begin to understand this, they will be better able to put themselves in the position of another. Once your partner can understand how another person feels, they will be more likely to help them.

Don't Take Life So Seriously

To someone with narcissism, not getting their way seems like a life and death situation. But examining what happens if the narcissist doesn't get their way can make it easier to understand that horrible things will most likely not happen.

The narcissist needs to remind themselves that they are not perfect and they do not have to be. They need to look for the humor in little things. As soon as they learn not to take life so seriously, humor can be found. And tomorrow, it probably won't even be that important. Once your partner realizes that even though yesterday seemed like a life and death situation, it's not the same as the present situation and so it will become easier to not take things so seriously, to laugh at their own mistakes, and to move forward in a more loving way. When everything is no longer about them and they face the fact that they cannot get everything they wanted and learn that it is not a crisis, things will get easier. They will learn to let go of these things and to move on more easily. Your partner will learn that they do not have to have control of everything. Life will not fall apart.

Practice Self-Compassion

This is especially true if your narcissist is the grandiose type, but it is more important to practice self-compassion rather than develop self-esteem. Your narcissistic partner already has plenty of confidence, and this is what makes them think they are entitled to everything they want and desire. Instead, fostering self-compassion will also help promote tenderness for other people. And, in the end, this is what will cause your partner to change their behavior, by understanding that everyone deserves love and respect. It starts with loving and respecting themselves.

To foster self-compassion, consider the three steps namely, developing self-kindness, understanding our common humanity, **and** practicing mindfulness.

Self-kindness is the simple idea that we should not beat ourselves up when something goes wrong. It means that when we talk to ourselves in our mind, it should be kind, rather than harsh. If you or your partner makes a mistake, what thoughts go through your mind? Do you berate yourself or do you try to comfort yourself? Most narcissists will berate themselves, and then lash out to try and make they feel better. Instead of lashing out at themselves, they should practice saying kind things in their mind. Remind yourself that everyone makes mistakes and that it's okay not to be perfect because no one is. Say nice things to yourself.

Second, realizing that everyone faces the same struggles will help to connect to that common bond that we call humanity. Everyone has imperfections. Everyone feels insecure at times and everyone has problems. When you practice self-compassion, you put yourself on the same level with everyone else around you. This is a necessary step for the narcissist. When they are able to do this, they can stop treating everyone else as if they are only meant to serve their needs. They will realize that they are part of a greater whole, not above it. This will make it easier for them to change their behaviors. This is the key realization to turn a narcissist into a loving human being; that everyone comes from the same place and has issues from various roots. No one's problems or ideas are more important than another's.

Lastly, the narcissist must learn to practice mindfulness, which means keeping your thoughts in the present moment. It also means acknowledging your feelings as they happen and thus deal with them. By suppressing what one thinks and feels, it will cause emotional outbursts later. By dealing with them in the present moment, the narcissist will be less likely to act out in negative ways.

By working through these steps, the narcissist can be turned into a thoughtful and loving person. Self-compassion, when practiced regularly, will naturally transform into compassion for the world around them. It will need much effort and will take time. Doing these things is not an easy, but the benefits for both the narcissist, and you, as the partner, will be immensely gratifying.

DEALING WITH EMOTIONAL ABUSE

If you or your partner find these steps quite difficult, it can be useful to seek professional help. A therapist or counselor can be an impartial guide to following these steps, can provide essential insight that you both missed, and can make sure that the two of you are not seeking to hurt each other, even unintentionally. Although not necessary, a therapist can be a valuable asset in the quest of turning your narcissist partner into an unselfish, loving partner.

It is my sincere hope that you and your partner are both willing to put the work necessary in your relationship to improve it. By following the techniques laid out in this book, you can have the person you love turn into a thoughtful, unselfish partner. But they, too, have to be willing to do the work. Remember, you cannot force someone to change. You can change how you act, but if your partner is not willing to engage in the work laid out in this chapter, there is only so much you can do to improve your relationship. But, working together, you and your partner can accomplish miraculous things. You can get the loving partner you want and he or she can learn to deal with life and relationships more effectively.

CHAPTER 10: HOW CAN YOU HELP A NARCISSISTIC PERSON?

A narcissist is never going to be a good support person for you. However, you do need support when you are dealing with someone like this in your life. If they are close to you and have been in your life a while, the first step is learning what a healthy relationship is. It is about mutual respect and give and take. With a narcissist, you only give, and they only take.

YOU CANNOT SAVE ANYONE

Focus your time on those that give you love, respect, and honesty. This will help you to see who you truly are so that you do not have to get approval from the narcissist in your life.

Start to break away from the person. A narcissist wants all attention on them, so they often try to isolate those they want to keep to themselves. This makes it easier for them to gain control over you. Spend time meeting new people or reconnecting with friends you might have lost touch with.

Seek out meaningful opportunities and activities. Consider going for that promotion you have wanted, volunteer or try a new hobby. When you have a fulfilling life, this acts as a natural support system for you.

How to Treat a Narcissist

You want to start by distinguishing between a grandiose narcissist and a vulnerable one. When you are dealing with one that is vulnerable, they have a weak inner core that they are masking with outward self-absorption and self-centeredness. The grandiose ones are not shy about how great they believe they are and they truly believe that they are the best.

Treating a narcissist in the right way is the easiest method for ensuring that their negative behavior does not fall back on you and cause negativity in your life. To ensure that you are treating them in the right way, there are a number of things you want to do so that you can evaluate them and develop the best strategy.

Determine the Narcissist's Type

You want to know if you are dealing with a vulnerable or grandiose narcissist. This makes it possible to determine what is needed to get the best response from them. For example, the grandiose type feels they are the best, so they need their ego stroked. On the other hand, the vulnerable type needs to feel special at all times due to their fragile ego. They need constant praise and reassurance.

Acknowledge How Annoyed You Are

Narcissists can really get under your skin, and this can cause you to be annoyed with them. They want all of the attention, so they commonly interrupt you when you are doing anything other than giving them attention. Do not just blow this off. Instead, acknowledge that their behavior annoys you so that you can start putting a stop to it.

Consider the Context

In many cases, certain situations are what trigger the worst of a narcissist's behavior. For example, you have a coworker who desperately wanted a promotion, but someone else got it. If she is a narcissist, this rejection can cause her to become very insecure, and in some cases angry. This would result in her becoming spiteful, vindictive and downright difficult to deal with.

Know the Source of the Behavior

A narcissist does not think like everyone else. For those without narcissism, getting over insecurities is not overly difficult. It is just a part of healthy coping. However, with a narcissist, they essentially need to have their ego rebuilt after a situation that caused them to feel inferior. It is important to balance how you treat them after a tough time. For example, you are working on a school project with someone who is a narcissist. Something happens that exposes a weakness in them. This breaks their ego and can make them just stop working on the project, but you still need their contribution. To get them back on track, you have to give them balanced reassurance. Too much and their ego can quickly get too big again, so approach the situation with this in mind.

Do Not Allow the Narcissist to Derail You

When you are doing something that takes attention from them, they might try to sabotage you so that you stop doing it and get back to making them number one. It is important that you keep your goal upfront and do not allow anything that they do or say to stop you from pursuing your goal or doing what you want to do. For example, you and a narcissist usually do something together on Friday nights. However, you decide that you want to start taking a class on your own. Since this takes your attention away from them, they may try to do things to get you to quit taking your class. Do not give in.

Make Sure to Stay Positive

Narcissists feed on watching other people feel bad, so even if they do cause you to experience negative emotions, do not let them see this. When you are around them, make sure that you are in a positive mindset. No matter how hard they try to bring you down, keep a smile on your face and do not react to them.

Call Their Bluff

Remember that they want to keep you down because this makes it easier for them to control you. When they are trying to do something negative, do not give in and do not get offended. Instead, walk away or laugh. They want to see you upset, so if you do not do this in front of them, it starts to take away some of their control.

Know That They Need Help

Narcissism is a mental health issue that someone cannot just will away. They will need help if they ever expect to get their behavior under control. If you approach them and recommend they reach out to a professional, they are unlikely to just agree and go. They may even become angry or defensive due to you even suggesting it. If you care about the person and want them to at least consider help, approach the subject gently and know that this is something that you will likely have to discuss several times before they will even consider it.

ARE NARCISSISTS DANGEROUS?

Being able to identify a narcissist is just the beginning. Once you recognize that you have one in your life, the next step is knowing how to overcome the experiences and any associated consequences. It can be emotionally and mentally challenging to be around a person with narcissism. It is imperative to not delay dealing with the situation properly to minimize the potential negative effects.

Dealing with a Narcissist

Dealing with a narcissist is something that truly takes practice. They are different than those without narcissism, and since this is not an issue that you deal with frequently with multiple people, there is a learning curve. The most important thing is to never discount yourself for them. This is what they want, but there are ways to recognize this and ensure that you are creating and maintaining the right boundaries.

Do Not Give Into Their Fantasy

A narcissist builds a fantasy life, and when dealing with them, it is important to not fall for the fantasy. They can be charming so it can be hard to resist them. It does not take long to essentially get lost in their web. At first, you might feel important special and important to them, but this never lasts. Keep the following in mind concerning not falling for the fantasy:

- They will not fulfill your needs. In fact, what you need and want will not even be recognized, so it is important to keep this in mind. A narcissist views your value as what you can do for them and what you can do to satiate their ego.

- Pay close attention to how they treat other people. You will be able to see that they are not afraid to manipulate, lie, disrespect and hurt other people. Eventually, this behavior and treatment will trickle down to you.

- While it is not easy, the rose-colored glasses have to come off. It is not easy to really evaluate how they are truly treating you, but it is important that you do this. When you care about someone, denial is the easiest route to take concerning their true character, but this has to be put aside for you to deal with a narcissist in the best way possible.

- Make sure that you do not forget about your dreams. When you are close to a narcissist, it is easy to get swept up in their delusions and fantasy. It is important that you do not lose yourself in this or else you may find it hard to regain control over who you are.

Set Your Boundaries and Stick to Them

One of the biggest elements of a healthy relationship is setting healthy boundaries and sticking to them. Of course, a narcissist does not understand boundaries, so this can be tricky. Remember that your relationships with others should be built on a foundation of mutual respect and care. While you will not get what you give, you still have to approach the relationship like you will. This will reduce the chances of your boundaries being violated.

For example, a narcissist is not shy about taking what they want. You might have a female friend who is a narcissist that just raids your closet when she wants to and takes anything. In a normal friendship, this friend would ask first, but narcissists do not ask permission. They feel that they deserve anything that they want, and this includes anything that you have that they might want.

If you have had a relationship with a narcissist for a while, you surely can see their pattern of not respecting your boundaries. To change this, make a plan. This plan should be based on what you hope to achieve by making it. Then, consider how you will enforce the plan and what the consequences will be should the narcissist violate your boundaries. The most important thing about your plan is that you stand firm and that you do not give into the needs of the narcissist. Make sure to let them know when your boundaries have been crossed.

Be prepared for relationship changes. A narcissist is not a big fan of people not admiring them and giving into their every whim. They want to call all of the shots, and they want you to prop them up. Once you start creating boundaries, how they treat you is likely to change because they will not be happy about you standing up for yourself. They may try to punish you, demean you, or they might go in the opposite direction and use fake charm to try and manipulate you into going back to give them what they want.

If you want to do what you can to maintain the friendship, you might take a gentle approach to boundary setting. For example, instead of just abruptly changing things and being harsh when explaining why, plan what you want to say and then deliver the message in a way that is clear, calm, gentle and respectful. If the conversation is not going as planned, simply walk away. Do not continue to engage or allow the person to try to manipulate you into going back into your old habits of just giving into them.

Avoid Taking Things Personally

This will be one of the hardest things that you do, but it is important. A narcissist is not purposely trying to hurt you. This is just who they are, and they are unable to see fault in their behavior. Remember that their actions, behaviors, and emotions are not about you. This is all about them.

A narcissist will try to create a version of you that is easiest for them to control. It is important that you work on your self-esteem and know your worth so that their view of you does not become how you see yourself. Let them keep their own negativity and do not allow it to change how you feel about yourself.

This also means that you need to know who you are. A narcissist is not able to admit that they have weaknesses and they overinflate their strengths. However, you need to take an honest look at yourself. If a narcissist is attacking one of your strengths, you can simply walk away. You know it is something that you are good at. Be proud of it and do not allow them to make you feel inferior.

Do not argue with them. This will be hard when the natural instinct is to defend yourself when someone is attacking you. Remember that a narcissist is not rational and no amount of logic you use to defend your point will change this. Simply state calmly that you disagree and then walk away.

Lastly, never look to a narcissist for approval. Even if they do tell you nice things, they are only doing it to manipulate and gain control over you. As long as you know your worth and have good self-esteem, you do not need them to approve of anything you do or think.

Freeing Yourself from Negative Emotions

Anger, jealousy, envy and other negative emotions can permeate your life and cause significant problems. It is important to recognize their existence and then work to be free of them. Freeing yourself from such emotions is a process, and it takes time. Even after you free yourself, you will need to commit to long-term work and maintenance.

Negative emotions are powerful and can quickly become habits if you do not get them under control. For example, if you commonly respond to criticism with anger, over time, this repetition will cause you to become angry any time you are criticized. This can start to impact your relationships, your career and other elements of your life.

Stop Justifying

The first step is to stop justifying your negative emotions. If you are getting angry all of the time, take responsibility for why and stop trying to place the blame elsewhere. Anger is a very powerful emotion, and it can quickly become a habit. As soon as you recognize that this habit is problematic and admit that it is not good, you can start to reevaluate why you are feeling this way so that you can change it.

Stop Making Excuses

When you make excuses for negative emotions, either for yourself or others, you are telling yourself that they are something out of your control. This is not true because you have the choice concerning how you react to a situation. If you continue to make excuses, you will never take responsibility for your behavior. Over time, this can start to push people out of your life because they will not want to be around someone who cannot admit their faults or when they are wrong.

Take Responsibility

Once you dedicate yourself to no longer making excuses, you can start to take some responsibility for how you act in various situations. This starts by taking the power away from your negative emotions. As you continue to take responsibility, you will find that they lose their hold over you. The right reactions and choices will naturally start to become easier to make.

Do Not Overanalyze Other People's Opinions of Your

Your emotions are your responsibility, but external factors can make them a bit harder to control. One of the biggest external factors is how other people view you. This is especially true if someone is especially vocal in criticizing you. This is often what narcissists do to try and keep you under their control.

Humans naturally want to be wanted and loved. When someone you respect or care about says something negative about you, the natural reaction is to go on the offensive. However, you want to instead hear what they are saying and then determine if it is true. For example, did your supervisor yell at you for making a small error on a work project? Consider why they yelled. Think about the big picture. Okay, you made a small mistake, but overall, you completed the project and did well with it. Remember this and allow the yelling to roll off your back.

Stop Your Bad Habits

Any bad habit you have can add to the negatively in your life. For example, eating fast food often, smoking or not maintaining good dental hygiene. Take a little time to write down the bad habits that you have. Once you put them in writing, they are easier to recognize. Start by working on one at a time because it is easier to correct a bad habit when you can put a lot of focus on it. When you work to enhance your total well-being, your emotions will benefit.

Cut Off Negative People

If there are people in your life that are largely a negative influence, walk away. It does not matter how close you are or how long you have known the person. When they are constantly negative, this is not doing anything good for your life. If you really care about the person, you can consider talking to them. However, not everyone can change, and some may just not want to. For example, a narcissist is not able to just stop their negative behavior. It is a part of their personality. Because of this, just talking to them is not likely to get you anywhere.

Think Before Responding

Negative emotions are powerful, so it is not uncommon for them to just spill out. However, train yourself to wait 10 seconds before responding to a situation that causes you to have negative emotions. This allows you to calm down so that your response is appropriate for the situation. For example, you were supposed to meet a friend for dinner, and you were an hour late. They are upset. Instead of just responding back in anger and getting into a fight, count to 10 and then consider why they are mad. It will be easier to see that they did nothing wrong and that you should apologize.

Be Grateful

Even during the worst of times, you have things in your life that are awesome that you should be grateful for. When you put your focus on these instead of the negative, it helps to alleviate the negative feelings. You might consider keeping a journal and then at the end of each day, take a few minutes to write down all of the good things that happened that day. Over time, the positive elements of your life will start to naturally outweigh the negative.

Stop Saying, "I Can't"

If you keep telling yourself that you cannot do something, you will eventually start to believe it. This is what is referred to as a self-fulfilling prophecy. Give yourself credit and stop limiting yourself to what is easy and in your comfort zone. As you push yourself and see how many things you are truly good at, this puts you in a more positive frame of mind, naturally pushing out the negative emotions.

Let It Go

Life would be much simpler if everything could be controlled, but this is not possible. When you find something that you have no control over, recognize it and let it go. For example, not every person will like you, and there are times when a loved one may get mad at you for something that is not your fault. Do not press the issue. Let it go, and everything will eventually work itself out in the end.

There are simpler things that you can start doing on a regular basis to start pushing out negative emotions and helping to enhance your overall well-being. You do not have to do every single one on a daily basis but consider them and incorporate them into your day when it is appropriate. These include:

- Get proactive and do not allow the negative to just settle into your life

- When life gets tough, cry it out because this can aid in reducing stress

- Scream as loud as you can for a few seconds as this naturally counteracts negative emotions

- Get some sleep since it is easier to tackle stress and negative emotions when you are not exhausted

- Try to be positive and no matter what happens, force yourself to find the silver lining in the situation

- Take a few minutes to laugh every day since when you are laughing, negative emotions cannot be present

- Find someone you trust who care about you and talk to them when you need to get help with a problem

- Consider an alternate perspective to see if it might allow you to better solve a problem

- Forgive yourself for setbacks as long as you recognize them and do not allow them to completely throw you off track

- Own your feelings and when negative emotions occur, recognize them, consider why you are experiencing them and then detach from it

- Write about the day or experience you just had before going to bed each night because this allows you to leave the negative in the past so you can start fresh the next day

CHAPTER 11: DATING AFTER LEAVING A NARCISSIST

When your relationship has not reached such a toxic point and you don't really see any severe warning signs, there may be hope for saving the relationship. There are treatments and techniques for managing narcissistic personality disorder. These will be discussed in more detail in the next chapter. Here we will discuss strategy you yourself can use to live with a narcissist and help them overcome this personality disorder so that you can have a loving and nurturing relationship with each other.

So, if your relationship has not yet reached its critical breaking point, here are some things you can try in order to make life with your partner more enjoyable and satisfying for the both of you.

- Identify the problem: if you are reading this book, you have already begun to work on this step. Look for the key traits that characterize a narcissist and decide if those apply to your partner. Then, read more about narcissistic personality disorder so that you understand not only the symptoms but the causes and treatment options. Learn as much as you can and then look for more to learn. Realize that this is a real problem that needs to be addressed.

- Do not be an enabler: once you know what the problem is and how the narcissistic personality disorder operates; you will be better prepared to deal with it. If you notice your partner acting in a narcissistic way (i.e.- acting arrogant, self-absorbed, or ignoring your needs and feelings), confront the problem rather than allowing it to continue or catering to it. Even if it seems easier at the time to just let it go; doing so will only allow the problem to become worse until it is too late and you have no option but to get out or suffer.

- Set firm boundaries: since narcissists tend to put their own needs before anyone else's, it is likely that your needs are beginning to fall by the wayside. You need to stop this process dead in its tracks. First, learn to distinguish between the legitimate needs and desires your partner has and the delusional or unrealistic ones. Then make it very clear for your partner what they can and cannot demand from you. Tread carefully here since narcissists are overly sensitive to criticism. Make sure to point out that you do love your partner and that you are willing to meet his or her needs. But only when those needs are genuine and realistic. You also need to make it clear that you expect the same in return from your partner.

- Avoid one-sided conversations: narcissists have difficulties with empathy and, if allowed, will steer every conversation into a discussion about themselves. They only want to talk about their needs and desires. While it is important to let your partner express his or her needs and desires, it is equally important that you have the space to express yours as well. If the conversation starts to become predominantly about your partner, balance it out and bring it back to yourself so that it becomes a two-sided conversation.

- Avoid blaming yourself: narcissists can be manipulative and may make you feel guilty for not allowing them to indulge in their narcissistic behaviors. Do not, on any account, allow yourself to feel guilty or blame yourself. Point out that your needs are also important. Explain that you respect his or her needs but that this relationship needs to be a give and take. If he or she really struggles with empathy, set out clear guidelines for how he or she can practice empathy. Do not play into their attempts at making you feel guilty.

- Avoid anger: in arguments, it is easy to become angry very quickly. This is particularly the case with narcissists who tend to fly off the handle quickly.

When one person in an argument is angry, it makes the other one angry. Try to resist this and remain calm. Understand that this anger is coming from your partner's inability to healthily deal with conflict. If you also get angry, it will only make your partner angrier and less capable of rationally dealing with the issue. Maintain calm so that you can maintain control of the situation. The more often your partner sees that you maintain calm even in these arguments; the more he or she will realize that you are not going to lose control of the situation or back down from your position no matter what they do.

- Get professional help: this is absolutely essential. Unless you are a trained therapist or psychiatrist yourself, you cannot deal with narcissistic personality disorder on your own. If your partner is unwilling to see a therapist—since doing so would mean acknowledging that he or she has a problem, something a narcissist cannot do—suggest couples therapy and frame the problem as a relationship issue rather than strictly an issue with your partner.

As you work through couples therapy, your partner will likely grow more and more willing to seek one-on-one therapy where he or she will be able to dig deeper down to the root of the problem. Furthermore, couples therapy can help provide you a safe space to address your issues with your partner. With a trained therapist in the room, it will be easier to keep control of the situation because the therapist will know how to handle your narcissistic partner.

CHAPTER 12: THE FUTURE FOR A NARCISSIST WHO REFUSES HELP

This ultimately comes down to knowing your worth and putting up your boundaries with any narcissist you might meet in the future. With improved self-esteem and knowing how to approach those who are narcissistic, you can better avoid falling into their web and having your life filled with their negativity.

First and foremost, make a pact with yourself that you will never allow another narcissist to take control over you. You are valuable, and your worth is determined by you and not them. They can quickly worm their way into your life because they are charming. It is easy to not believe a narcissist is actually a narcissist at first. They can be initially nice, or at least seem that way based on their actions and their desire to control and manipulate you.

Consider your past experience with a narcissist. Do you remember how the relationship began? Look for similar patterns with any new person in your life who you think might be a narcissist. Remembering history is one of the best ways to prevent issues from your past from repeating themselves. It can be hard to spot the signs at first, so be diligent and do not discount your feelings if you think another narcissist has entered your life.

Go to your support system and people you trust. Ask their opinion about the person you think might be a narcissist. In many cases, when you are getting close to someone, it can be difficult to see their flaws. However, your close friends and family are on the outside looking it and can pick up on issues faster and easier than you can. Just remember that if their opinions are negative, do not get defensive. They care about you and want to ensure that you are surrounded by good people.

Practice regular self-care. When you are taking care of yourself and putting yourself first, you are less vulnerable to the charms and manipulations of a narcissist. There are numerous ways to practice self-care. You can choose one or several methods depending on your needs and what you want. The following are common self-care methods to consider:

- Make your schedule simpler so that you can put more focus on the activities that make you happy and alleviate your stress.

- Take a warm bath and use this time to read a book, listen to your favorite songs or just kick back. Make sure the atmosphere is relaxing and that this is time just for you. Turn off your phone and eliminate any distractions.

- Get some physical activity since this will help to boost your physical, mental and emotional health. It is a good way to blow off some steam. Any type of physical activity that you enjoy will provide you with benefits.

- Create a list of what you are grateful for. A narcissist can take away your joy, so sometimes you need to remind yourself of the things in your life that are great.

- Find a mentor that can aid you in getting to know yourself and guide you through difficult times. This can be a religious leader, a therapist or any person in this realm.

- Take a day to unplug from everything. Turn off all electronics and go back to a simpler time. Take a walk or a nap, enjoy favorite foods, play games with friends or anything else that does not require electronics.

- Try something new. Have you been wanting to start painting or write a book? Is there a type of cuisine you have not tried before? As long as it is something new to you, do it. This gets you out of your comfort zone and expands your horizons.

- Go dancing. Just like physical activity, dancing can alleviate stress, and it contributes to greater well-being. Hit a club with friends or just crank up some tunes in your living room and dance it out.

- Get out in nature. It is true that nature has a way to make you feel calmer and more relaxed. It is also quiet and allows you to engage in self-reflection. A quick walk or hike is a good place to start.

- Learn how to meditate. Even just five minutes of meditation per day can help to keep you grounded and it makes it easier to deal with stressors.

- Start a journal to keep track of your thoughts and feelings.

- Eliminate the clutter in your living space. When your home is more organized and clean, this helps to make you calmer. Clutter naturally induces feelings of stress.

- Make sure to get adequate sleep. Get yourself on a regular sleeping schedule and stick to it. If you want to take a nap during the day, keep it to an hour or less so that it does not interfere with your ability to sleep at night.

CHAPTER 13: ARE MODERN SOCIAL ELEMENTS TO BLAME?

You almost know all there is to know about narcissists and the issues and traits that go with it. We also need to look at another area. Are social elements to blame for the increasing number of narcissists?

True narcissists are very rate but it is a term that we hear more and more. For this reason, narcissistic behaviors are more common now, so we need to find out why? Is it all the social pressures we have to deal with? Is it social media? Is it because we are pressured to own the best, look, the best, and be the best?

It is unfair to put the blame of narcissism at modern society's feet. It does make one wonder if it did have a hand in it. Social media makes us aware of the way other people live and look. The influences of social media tell us that if we want to be the best, we must look our best, and this means we have to use a certain product. We get bombarded with people constantly taking selfies and full body photos and then using filters and photoshop to change their appearance drastically. The majority of what we see just isn't real. Now, do you wonder why we have all these unrealistic expectation of what we should look like, what we should be, and what we need to aim for?

No one is completely sure what causes narcissism, so it is the things we are exposed to in life? Most of the narcissistic cases are thought to come from things we experienced during childhood, but what caused those experiences? What makes someone act a specific way? What makes someone create trauma to another human that can cause them to develop a certain personality disorder? It is hard to figure out, but you have to take into account all the possibilities.

We might not completely understand what causes narcissism, and there is a specific amount of stigma attached to it. If we try to be the best, it will be a constant, fruitless task. We should try to just be ourselves.

When talking about future generations, it is our responsibility to make sure our children are brought up to be happy just being who they are, without have to constantly compete to reach unrealistic goals. If we can do this, we are going to raise a generation of young people who are fulfilled, respectful, and well-mannered. These are great boosts toward avoiding trauma and personality disorders.

CONCLUSION

The next step is to work to apply the information to your life. You know that while dealing with narcissism is not easy, it is certainly an experience that you can cope with and find a positive outlook for.

Knowing more about what might feed a narcissistic personality gives you a greater insight into how to deal with those around you who may have it. Once you can identify the traits, behaviors, and emotions, you have a better handle on essentially what makes the person tick.

You now know more about exactly what defines a narcissist and the people they may be. With this information, it is easy to see that a narcissist can be someone you consider a friend, a mentor or even a person you are in a deeper relationship with.

After determining the narcissists that surround you, dealing with them properly becomes key. It is important that you utilize the information here so that you can interact with them in the healthiest way possible. The anger, envy, and other negative emotions will not help you even though they are a natural reaction to such behavior.

Lastly, you now know that your personal self-esteem is important. When you are confident, it not only makes it easier to identify a narcissist but also to better cope with them. You can handle such behavior in a way that does not have a profoundly negative impact on your life.

It is inevitable that you will run into a narcissist at least once in your life. Just remember that you do not have to just deal with them. There are ways to healthily cope with their behavior so that your self-esteem and life do not take a major negative hit.

HEALING FROM NARCISSIST EMOTIONAL ABUSE:

BUILDING YOUR

SELF-ESTEEM AND RECOVERING

YOURSELF

[Gloria Newton]

Introduction

Have you ever been with your partner and felt a sense of dread even in the most innocent of situations? You may not have known why, but a certain level of uneasiness may have settled over you, coloring your mood as you watched your partner go about his or her routine?

If this sounds familiar, you may be in a relationship with a narcissist. Narcissists are people who seek to absorb as much as they can from other people with little regard for how the other person may be doing. All attention must be on them and they do not care how their desires hurt others.

If you have a narcissist in your life, you are likely feeling blindsided by the abuse you may suffer, doubting yourself and your own sanity at times due to the narcissist's charisma and manipulation. It is important for you to know, however, that you do not have to feel that way.

The following chapters will discuss all the things that you need to know in order to deal with the issues and the harm that can happen with narcissistic abuse.

This guidebook is going to take some time to talk about narcissistic abuse and some of the things that we need to know about it. Take some time to look through this guidebook to learn more about what you can do if you end up falling into a relationship with a narcissist and dealing with narcissistic abuse.

The truth is that narcissists are all around us. Indeed, it has been alleged that narcissism may actually be on the rise, which is an assertion that seems to be gaining support, especially as incidents of online abuse and bullying become more common and more talked about.

The best first step in defending against narcissistic abuse is understanding what it is. The narcissist may act without regard to your feelings, but he or she is able to get a read on them. The narcissist may have a goal that causes them to disregard your feelings, or they may derive pleasure from tormenting you.

Interacting with a narcissist will be fraught with danger because you will never be certain whether the person you are dealing with is using against you what you tell them or what you share with them emotionally. Narcissism can impact your relationships in ways that you may not recognize. Narcissistic abuse does not have to be the end of you. And fighting back does not mean that you have to begin behaving narcissistically too. Once you understand narcissistic behavior as part of a pattern of disordered behaviors, you will learn how to protect yourself better.

Chapter 1: Understanding Narcissistic Abuse

Abuse comes in all sorts of forms, the vast majority of which never leave a single physical mark on the victim. These various forms of abuse all still lead to the same result: The victim suffering at the hands of his or her abuser. No matter the form, this sort of treatment is not acceptable nor should it be allowed to happen. The first and foremost signal to yourself that you are suffering from dealing with a narcissist in a toxic relationship is the persistent feeling that you are alone. If you come home each day and see your boyfriend, eat meals with your boyfriend, sit in front of a TV with your boyfriend, then go to bed next to a boyfriend, but still feel like you've spent the whole day alone, it's because you might be dealing with a narcissist who is only presenting to you a mirage of the relationship you thought you were living. There is an absence of feeling underneath the actions that leave you feeling lost, confused, and very lonely. If you feel this constantly and are unsure of where the feeling came from, this may be a sign of narcissistic abuse syndrome.

Types of Narcissistic Abuse

Physical Abuse

This is what most people think of when they consider abuse. Physical abuse involves punishments through physical means. Anything that leaves physical harm on your body, whether it leaves a mark on you or not, is physical abuse. If there is ever a moment in which the other party has laid a hand upon you or touched you in any way when you did not consent or want that touch, it is considered physical abuse and should not be tolerated. Ultimately, your body is your own to govern and if you do not want to be touched, you have the right to decide that.

Verbal Abuse

Whenever the voice is involved in a way that is mean to hurt or demean you, you are being verbally abused. This includes comments that are meant to hurt, such as belittling, disparaging remarks, or yelling at you. While some people may say things that are critical but to use them in a legitimate manner to help better you, the narcissist uses his voice to keep you down. Oftentimes, verbal abuse goes ignored because it does not leave a mark on you but the constant name-calling or insults can wear down on you and do lasting damage to your mental welfare.

Verbal abuse includes any sort of verbal harm, such as threats, demands, guilt trips, sarcasm, yelling, calling names, insulting, or anything else that involves the voice that you consider intentional and harmful.

Sexual Abuse

Also, one of the most insidious, damaging forms of abuse one can inflict upon another, sexual abuse involves the forced sexual acts or sexual touches without consent. This does not have to be full intercourse; even simply touching you in ways that make you uncomfortable or tapping your butt without your consent would be considered a form of sexual abuse.

Remember, just because you may be in a relationship with or married to the other person does not give him or her a free pass to use your body in ways you are not comfortable with. A spouse can absolutely sexually abuse the other party if it is not consensual. Remember, someone under the influence of drugs or alcohol cannot consent to sexual contact nor can someone who is sleeping. Forcing the point and badgering you into sex that you do not want is also considered a form of sexual abuse.

Financial Abuse

When you are a victim of financial abuse, you are restricted from money somehow. Particularly common in abusive marriages, this often involves one person who stays home and one person who earns all of the money, though this is not always the case.

One person takes control of all of the money and restricts access to it, regardless of who earns it. The entire point is to keep the dependent stuck, relying on the abuser to provide for all of his or her needs.

Frequently, this is done by using multiple bank accounts to restrict access, providing the victim either with nothing at all or only small stipends of money at a time to cover basic necessities while withholding the rest. The abuser may have taken control of your finances through theft, forcibly taking your access to money and limiting it, or simply moving all funds into an account you have no access to. It can also be done through taking out credit cards in your name and using them to accrue debt and keep you trapped. If you do not have equal access to the money in a marriage and have not agreed to that arrangement, you may be a victim of financial abuse. Of course, some couples agree to split finances, but that must be a mutual decision.

Emotional Abuse

Emotional abuse is intended to hurt you emotionally, as the name implies. It involves threats to keep you in line, using the silent treatment to hurt you, belittling you, or using the favored love bomb and devalue cycle or FOG. The purpose of this is to toy with your emotions for no reason other than to entertain the narcissist. Most attempts at manipulation fall into this category, as they attempt to sway you by appealing to emotions.

Isolation

Isolation involves intentionally restricting access to other people that may be a form of support for the victim. This includes making it so other people take little interest in approaching the victim, such as making it so uncomfortable for the victim's friends and family to visit that they eventually decline to do so, or by restricting contact through social media. If the narcissist insists that you cut off certain people if you want to continue the relationship, he or she is likely isolating you.

Signs of Narcissistic Abuse

When you become repeatedly exposed to these types of abuse, you eventually begin to develop telltale signs of an abuse victim. Of course, not every person will follow this exact pattern or exhibit every single symptom on the list, and an absence of any of these symptoms does not automatically mean that the person is not being abused. Familiarize yourself with this list so you can recognize abuse in either yourself or in others.

Detaching or Dissociating

Dissociation is a form of coping mechanism in which you detach from your emotions. Oftentimes, your emotions are so overwhelming for you that you feel the need to detach from them altogether just to survive. This is commonly seen in people who have survived traumas, such as rape or war, and can also frequently be seen in the victims of narcissistic abuse. When this occurs, your mind is attempting to isolate the abuse as the only way it knows how to cope with the abuse, and can cause some serious mental health problems if left unchecked. It can lead to altered levels of consciousness and begin to affect your memory, as well as lead to serious health implications as well.

Distrusting Everyone

Due to encountering so much abuse by someone you once trusted and loved, you may become quite distrustful in response. You may constantly feel on edge, worried that you will be betrayed or hurt again, and your ability to make meaningful relationships may suffer. Instead, you remain hyper vigilant around other people, which only serves to heighten sensations of anxiety and drive wedges between yourself and other people. You likely suspect even those who you have never had a reason to distrust as being capable of harming you after your trauma.

Often or Always fearful

As a result of being so thoroughly betrayed, you may find yourself constantly fearing a repeat of the abuse. You may fear that your abuser will come back to you if you have escaped or you may worry that any happiness you find is a delusion. Because narcissists have a tendency to punish when someone around them is happy, you have likely repeatedly faced consequences to enjoying life, which as only served to make you worried whenever things go well. You constantly fear that the narcissist will be set off or that the other shoe will drop and your fragile moment of happiness will be shattered. You may develop a fear of enjoyment and because of this, you allow the narcissist to continue being the only one to enjoy anything. Of course, what the narcissist really enjoys is seeing his victims afraid of enjoying life.

Feeling of Walking on eggshells

Similar to being fearful, the feeling of walking on eggshells is that sensation you feel when you are desperately trying to tend to a delicate situation and you know that if you make the slightest mistake, no matter how harmless that mistake may seem, there will be a massive explosion. You live with that sensation constantly when with the narcissist; you feel as though she will explode on you at any given moment, even over things that are insignificant.

Martyring Yourself for others

Martyring yourself, in this case, refers to the act of making yourself suffer in order to benefit others. If you know that the narcissist wants muffins for breakfast but has not asked for them, for example, you might stay up late that night, making a batch from scratch to give to the narcissist, despite the fact that doing so means that you went to bed three hours late and are too exhausted to meet all of your responsibilities the next day. You may find other ways to do this, such as canceling an appointment to get your hair done that you had been looking forward to in order to take care of the narcissist's laundry or canceling some other thing you have been looking forward to for something that the narcissist is relatively indifferent about.

Self-guilt and Blame

With self-guilt, you seek to blame yourself for what you have gone through. You know that you are in a bad relationship with a narcissist and that you could have better but you feel as though you deserve it. You guilt yourself into staying, saying that the narcissist needs you, and that you are to blame for your suffering. You must not have tried hard enough if the narcissist is not doing better yet, and you need to try harder if you want the abuse to stop.

You may even begin to blame yourself for the narcissist's abuse, telling yourself that you had annoyed your abuser into punching you and if you are more careful in the future it will not happen. You make yourself responsible for the narcissist's actions and that train of thought only convinces you that you deserved it and that the abuse was justified.

Self-sabotaging

When self-sabotaging, you find ways to prevent yourself from succeeding. Oftentimes, this is related to the narcissist destroying your self-esteem. You begin to believe what the narcissist is saying about your capabilities and act them out. If you are repeatedly told that you are unintelligent, you will begin to believe it, and you will make choices that reflect that. You may be quite bright, but your own choices will be made based off of your sense of self-worth. Self-sabotaging could also take forms such as making it impossible for yourself to leave the relationship when you want to by failing to take the steps necessary to grant yourself the independence you crave.

Impact of Abuse

After enduring abuse for so long, the victims often find themselves feeling long-lasting effects. Even after escaping the abuse, the victims may still show the telltale signs of someone who has endured toxic abuse. If you notice these signs in yourself, remember, this does not reflect poorly on you. You are not broken or irreparably ruined and scarred. You are a survivor. These are the wounds that will heal with time the longer you are away from the narcissist and are nothing to be ashamed of. With time and effort, you will eventually heal into the person you deserve to become. Remember, you are a survivor despite of the abuse, and the abuse does not define you.

Echoism

Echoism refers to the way that people melt away when exposed to constant abuse. Their sense of self fades away until all that is left is an echo, a faint reminder of who that person used to be before the narcissist caused them to disappear. The echo puts her needs last, develops a fear of having needs at all, and feels selfish when her needs are met. The narcissist has manipulated her into forsaking her own needs, projecting his own selfishness onto her to keep her in line. She stops caring about herself and the only thing that matters in life at that point is the narcissist.

Physical or Mental Health Problems

Those who have endured constant abuse also frequently encounter mental and physical health complications. As stress does have an impact on the human body, due to it raising the levels of cortisol and other stress hormones, which inevitably drain on the victim, he may find himself suffering from anxiety, depression, post-traumatic stress disorder, or a series of other mental health issues. Even leaving is not necessarily enough to assuage the damage that is done. You will have to work to heal the mental wounds before your physical body can begin to heal. Your hormone levels that have adjusted to high levels of stress and constant fight-or-flight mode will not recover while you are still in contact with the narcissist. Your physical and mental health will be at risk of harm until you do ultimately decide to leave.

Ultimately, your best chance at recovering from such insidious abuse is through leaving the narcissistic abuser altogether. If you do not get out, you will not be able to heal the wounds; they will be kept open through repeated injury until you eventually believe that you have no chance to get out or be happy.

Thoughts of Self-harm or Suicide

Along with mental health problems, you may find yourself constantly plagued with thoughts of self-harm, or sometimes even suicide. You may feel that life is not worth it at the hands of the narcissist. You might feel so ready for the abuse to end that you are willing to take matters into your own hands. If you are ever feeling as though you want to hurt yourself, you should treat this as a medical emergency and tell someone that you need real, immediate help. Medical professionals will be able to stabilize you until you can get further help.

Failure to Thrive in Future Relationships

This result is a culmination of all of the effects narcissistic abuse can have on you. Because of your past experiences and your distrustful nature, you may feel like you can never have a successful relationship again. You may feel as though you never want to make yourself vulnerable to another person again out of fear of being hurt, or you may feel so broken that you believe that you are not worth a proper, loving relationship. Remember, you should never try to jump into a relationship before you are ready, but you can go on to be in a healthy relationship if you so choose, especially if you take the steps to begin recovering from narcissistic abuse.

Chapter 2: Symptoms of Narcissistic abuse

For someone in a relationship with a narcissist, they feel an overwhelming sense of degradation. At the beginning of the relationship, the narcissist was charming, funny, very caring.

If you have ever been abused by a narcissist, there are going to be some symptoms that will prove that this happened. These symptoms are going to be pretty challenging to deal with. They often are going to result in some severe psychological trauma to those who have been in the relationship, and who have been abused, by the narcissist for some time.

You will find that there is going to be some early signs for this kind of abuse, and often they are going to arise after the initial love bombing stops and the narcissist decides that it is time to begin their cycle of destroying their victim. Of course, since these things start to happen early on, the victim will be full of energy and a lot of positivity, which means that the narcissist is going to be able to get away with quiet a bit without you even noticing. And they start out slow so you are less likely to notice what is going on here.

Questioning what is real

One of the major symptoms that will show up here is some memory problems. It is common that the victim of a narcissist is going to start doubting their own memory, or their own view of reality. Because of this, they are going to rely on the narcissist, and they hope that the narcissist is going to be able to feed them information on their reality.

Feeling like you are always on egg shells

Those who are dealing with narcissistic abuse are the ones who feel that they are living life on eggshells. This is going to be pretty common when it comes to people who have gone trough some kind of trauma in their relationship. It sometimes feels like you need to be careful so that you won't create a problem, so you, as the victim, will be careful about what you do and what you say around the narcissist

The victim will sacrifice themselves to make sure the abuser is happy.

If you are a victim in this relationship, it is very possible that you will find that you need to sacrifice a lot of things to make the abuser happy. It is common that the abuser will expect that you are going to give up your desires, needs, and sometimes safety.

The victim finds it hard to trust others

Because of the severe mental abuse that the victim is going to face from the narcissist, it is likely that the victim is going to feel like they are not able to trust anyone. Anyone who enters their lives will now turn into a threat to the victim. They may become anxious and will worry about the intentions of the other person. And often they will look at a situation and assume that the worst is going to happen each time.

The victim will blame themselves.

Narcissists have a great ability in order to take any blame that should belong to them, and shifting it so it goes to the victim. Because of this, the victim is conditioned in a way that they are going to take all of the responsibility when it comes to their actions and their behavior. The narcissist is going to blame the victim for making them upset, or doing something that they knew they were not supposed to do, and for a variety of other issues. The result of this is that the victim is going to constantly feel like they are responsible for actions, even if they are not sure how this happened, and like they are always the one who is responsible for things.

Feels almost like a love triangle.

Triangulation is going to be a prevalent tactic that narcissists are going to enjoy. The narcissist is able to do thy by creating a love triangle, bringing in a third party dynamic into the relationship so that you are terrorized even more than before. When they do this, the abuser is going to be able to promote the idea that the victim isn't good enough. The victim is then going to work in order to gain the attention and the love that they need and you will always work to gain the attention of the narcissist in order to get what they want.

The victim is afraid of being successful

People who find themselves in a relationship with a narcissism will find that the idea of being successful, especially if they are more successful than the narcissist, can be a problem. They know that the abuser is going to punish them for doing this. This is because the abuser is going to be envious about the success. They want to be the most successful, especially when it comes to being in that relationship. And if the victim is able to gain more success, then this throws off the balance that the narcissist thinks needs to be there.

The victim will be frequently sad or depressed

A healthy relationship should make you happy. If you are in a relationship where you frequently find yourself sad and depressed, and these feelings cannot be attributed to something outside of your relationship, then it may be time to take a long, hard look at why you are feeling this way. The sadness and depression you feel may be the result of emotional abuse, and even if you are not able to recognize the abusive acts, you may be able to notice how you feel.

The victim will be spending less time with friends and family

The narcissist seeks to isolate you because they want to control you, and they need you to enable their narcissism. Therefore, relationships with narcissists are frequently characterized by increased isolation from others that would normally be part of your circle. You may find yourself spending more and more time with the narcissist or at home. Less time is spent with friends and family. This does not have to be dysfunctional in a relationship necessarily, but when taken with the other signs, it can be a cause for concern.

They become anxious about interacting with their significant other

Your partner should make you feel safe. If you notice that you have anxiety when interacting with your partner, then this may indicate that there is an unhealthy aspect to this relationship. Sometimes, men and women in relationships can feel anxious because of something that they are doing, such as placing demands on their partner, but if your feelings of anxiety cannot be explained by any action of your own, then this is a sign that something is wrong.

The victim will feel exhausted for no reason

The emotional abuse of the narcissist can leave you feeling exhausted. A relationship with them can be an emotional rollercoaster of sorts, and the most visible marker of this ride is that you just feel exhausted. Exhaustion that cannot be satisfactorily explained by something else can be a sign that you are in a relationship with a narcissist.

The victim will find less joy in their accomplishments

The narcissist engages in emphasizing their own accomplishments and diminishing yours. If you find that things that caused you to feel happy or proud before no longer do that, then this may be a sign of the narcissistic abuse that you have been subjected to. The problem with this type of abuse is that you may subconsciously feel admiration for your partner, so you may not see the language that belittles you for the abuse that it is. Just keep in mind that your partner should make you feel better about yourself, not worse.

They behave in ways that run contrary to their interests

A narcissist can manipulate you into doing things that benefit him or her rather than yourself. They do this because they do not see your needs as being equal to their own, just as they do not see you as being equal to them in general. If you find that you act solely for the benefit of the narcissist, then you need to reevaluate your relationship seriously.

Part of you wants to leave the relationship, but you are too scared

It is only natural to want to leave a relationship where one feels the lasting effects of abuse. Although the decision of when or whether to leave always comes from the abused, the abused person often talks themselves out of leaving or is too scared to leave. If you often find yourself thinking about leaving the relationship but feel that you cannot, then this may be a sign that you are dealing with an abusive narcissist.

Chapter 3: How to heal from the abuse of a narcissist

Relationships are an important part of life. But with a narcissist, these relationships are toxic. A narcissist in a relationship makes everything seem dysfunctional to a point where we feel as if we have to be people who are slaves begging for love. They make us believe that we are getting the mental and physical abuse because we deserve it. We do not.

Being abused by a narcissist isn't something anyone should go through. We all deserve happiness, a life free from mental strain and the pull of manipulation that wraps itself around us and refuses to let go. We are the ones who have to let go.

You may feel suffocated by the relationship itself as your narcissist partner attempts to hijack your personal life and everything that existed before he/she entered your life.

The time that the healing process takes is not going to be set in stone. The time that it takes is going to vary from one victim to another. There are some times that you can step in and do in order to help promote this healing. These are going to be hard sometimes. And the longer that you were in that relationship, the harder it is going to be to work on these steps. But if you have found out that you were in a relationship with a narcissist, and you are ready to finally take care of yourself and heal, there are a few things that you can do to make it better.

The first thing to remember is that the healing trauma inside your brain is going to take some time, and it is going to present you with some challenges. Because of this, it is often not recommended that you try to work through this on your own. Seeking some kind of support is always the best thing to do, and you want to make sure that you pick out support that is caring, empathetic, and genuinely interested in helping you to heal. Finding friends, family, and even a therapist to walk through this with you will make a world of difference in how well you are able to deal with the relationship, and how likely it is that you will walk away.

Next, make sure that you spend some time getting rid of any toxicity that is present in your life. Since this experience is likely to have left you very isolated from others, taking the time to externalize can be helpful.

Doing the deep work here is going to be so important. Any time that we are abused, we are going to bring about a lot of damage inside. This is where you will need to stop and work through some of that inner trauma, and then heal everything that is inside of you. This is going to be hard, but spend some time going through all of the pieces of you that feel like they are broken, and then address these broken bits one by one.

This one is a good place to introduce a therapist to help you. They are able to listen to some of the thoughts and feelings that are going through your head, and then they will provide you with some support and advice when it comes to addressing the parts that seem to be really painful, but you just can't seem to let go. Some people also find that turning to spirituality helps them.

Get out there and volunteer, integrate yourself with the world that is out there, ask questions, and learn about others as much as you can. Get out into the world and make sure that you work on your own self-care, self-esteem, and self-confidence again.

Escaping and healing from this kind of relationship is going to be really hard for most victims to do. There are a lot of different parts that can keep the trapped in the relationship rather than letting them leave and be free the way that they want.

Steps to Healing from the Narcissistic Relationship

Even those who understand narcissism and what it entails may struggle to deal with the manipulation attempts. Though you may see the narcissist in action, if you do not understand how best to proceed in your interactions with the narcissist, you are still going to find yourself feeling the strains of her abuse. While the most surefire way to deal with abuse is to make it impossible to occur simply due to cutting off contact altogether, that is not always realistic or practical in real life. Sometimes, you have no choice but to maintain some semblance of contact with the narcissist, whether it is due to you having to co-parent together, or you have decided that you want to wait out your children becoming adults before freeing yourself from the abuse. Maybe your boss is a narcissist but you cannot afford to quit or find a new job. Regardless of the reason, there are a wide range of ways you can deal with a narcissist, ranging from cutting off to learning how to work with the narcissist's personality flaws. Remember, none of these are guaranteed to work for every single narcissist and it may take some trial and error before you figure out which methods will work best for you. However, in time, you will be able to work things out in a way that works for you. When you do learn how to deal with the narcissist's abuse tactics, however, you will likely discover the peace of mind that your life has been lacking ever since she managed to weasel her way into your life.

Acknowledge Your Abuse

Before you can begin to heal, you must first acknowledge what has happened. You must recognize that the narcissist in your life has harmed you, sometimes so much that you feel permanently ruined. Rest assured, none of the damage is permanent if you actively try to correct it, but you must start by calling what happened what it was: Abuse. You may have been taught to internalize it through long periods of being blamed for what happened and the narcissist gaslighting you into believing you are the problem and you must learn to separate yourself from the narcissist's actions. You did not deserve the abuse; the narcissist was abusive. That is not your flaw; it is the narcissists. You cannot control the narcissist's behavior, no matter how much you may wish you could or how much the narcissist may tell you it is your fault for provoking him, and by labeling it as abuse, you begin to accept that.

Healing begins with acknowledgment. If you cannot acknowledge that what the narcissist has put you through is abuse, you may not be ready for this process. By recognizing what happened as the abuse it was, you will be able to take the steps necessary to correct for it and heal. You will erase any of the denial you have hidden the abuse behind for however long it occurred by naming it.

Breaking the trauma bond

Breaking this bond is going to be a very important thing to do when you want to get out of a relationship that is abusive. It is sometimes challenging, but it is possible. The first step to work with is to decide exactly what you would like to live with, and that you actually want to live in reality and not with all of the lies that the abuser sends your way. it is also going to start with a denial of the illusions that you have been living with, including the ones that the abuser made for you, and any of the ones that you may have made for yourself.

Remember, even if you do love that person, they are an abuser, and they are not going to change it is fine if you need to take some time to grieve this process. Many victims agree that this letting go is going to feel like a real loss. You can grieve the loss of the person you thought you knew, but realize that this was a façade and that person never really existed. And then be fine with letting go.

Escape in a safe manner

The first thing that a victim needs to realize before they leave the relationship is that the narcissist is going to try to continue manipulating you. They want to bring you back to the relationship, not because they love you and need you but because they want and need the attention and adoration that you sent their way. They are going to try and get you back in a few different manners.

It is best, if you can at all, to leave cold turkey. There is going to be some pain that comes with it. You may feel that you is no one out there you can trust and talk to. But this is not true. You will be able to talk to a therapist, to your family members and more. And, once you have had some time to heal, despite what the narcissist said, you may find someone else who is worthy of your time and attention.

The no contact rule

To make sure that you are actually able to escape from the narcissist, it is important to enforce a rule of no contact. If you feel that this person is going to put you in serious danger, then having a legally enforced law surrounding this order could make a difference and will ensure that you are able to stay safe and sound the whole time.

If you do have any sort of communication with the narcissist at all, then you are allowing them back in and giving them the easy access that they need in order to manipulate you and make you stay in the relationship a bit longer. No matter what you think in the beginning, this is going to happen. If you do start to communicate with the narcissist, then they are going to use all of this information against you to bring you back, and then you have to start the process all over again. You have to remember that the whole abuse cycle left you weak and vulnerable, and it is much better for you if you can vanish away from the narcissist and focus on your own recovery.

Cut Ties With Narcissist

When you are plagued with abuse from a narcissist, and it is practical to do so, cutting off the narcissist is the most efficient thing you can do to end the abuse. If you are not married and do not cohabitate or share children, ending a relationship is simple enough. You can simply move on with your life and do your best to ignore the narcissist's desperate pleas to get you back. However, in choosing to cut off the narcissist, you are free to live the way you desire. You will be able to reclaim your life and avoid the problems that the narcissist has brought you.

When you do cut off the narcissist, you should keep in mind that you will still be subjected to the narcissist attempting to contact you. The reason for this behavior is because he is going through an extinction burst. In psychology, an extinction burst refers to a concept in which someone who has become accustomed to a certain kind of result for a specific behavior is suddenly denied the expected result and therefore tries to get the result by desperately trying to repeat the behavior with more and more frenzy.

Timeout From Narcissist

The goal of the timeout is not to punish the narcissist but instead to ensure that you are able take the time you need to evaluate the relationship with a level head so you make choices with a clear mind. Though the narcissist will be quick to accuse you of being abusive and manipulative, in true narcissistic projection fashion, you should not be swayed. Your actions are not to punish the narcissist but instead to care for yourself. You are engaging in self-care by taking a step back from a relationship that is causing you grief. That is not abusive.

Set Boundaries—and Keep Them

When contact does have to be maintained, recognize that you should set boundaries. Remember, healthy boundaries are absolutely essential for healthy relationships, and while you may never have a proper, healthy relationship with the narcissist, your boundaries will serve as barriers between yourself and the narcissist that will protect you from harm. These boundaries represent the clear line you draw between what is and is not acceptable to you. Everyone should have boundaries, including couples, as they create a baseline of expectations that you can work off of in order to ensure that you are not stepping on anyone's toes or unintentionally angering the other person. Most people will have no issues respecting your boundaries and will do so even if they disagree with whatever the boundary you set is.

The narcissist, however, does not respect boundaries. You know this—this is one of the ways they enjoy manipulating other people. When the narcissist inevitably intentionally violates your boundaries in some way or another, you should quickly correct her actions. Point out that you do not agree with whatever she has done, and say that if the behavior is repeated, you will do a specific consequence. When she inevitably tests the boundary again, you MUST enforce the consequence you said would apply.

Choose Your Deal-Breakers

These are things that are absolutely not okay with you and warrant an immediate cut-off. These are different than boundaries in the sense that they are so extreme. While your deal-breakers are essentially boundaries you have prioritized above all else, you will not give warnings for these. You will never allow the narcissist to attempt to test this boundary even once before deciding to instead cut off contact the first time it happens.

These boundaries should be things you are truly passionate about not encountering. In many relationships, the most clear-cut deal-breakers are affairs, abuse, and lying but your own may be different. If those are things that you would not tolerate in another relationship, do not tolerate it with the narcissist, no matter how much the narcissist may try to get you to give in. Your deal-breakers should remain deal-breakers no matter what.

Forgiveness and Compassion for Yourself

Forgive yourself for blaming yourself for the abuse so you can begin to celebrate those parts of yourself. You will be able to forgive yourself for not seeing the red flags when they happened, reminding yourself that your good nature may have been to see the good in everyone but ultimately the narcissist choosing to take advantage of that is not your fault.

You can forgive yourself for not leaving the relationship sooner, reminding yourself that you tried desperately to care for the narcissist, truly loving who he was, and that love was taken advantage of. Your good heart, your compassion and kindness when you see someone suffering, were taken advantage of. When you recognize that, you can forgive yourself.

Remember, forgiveness does not necessarily come easy but you deserve to forgive yourself. You did not intend for the situation to get as bad as it did and you are making an effort to heal the best that you can. You did your best in the situation with what you had, and that is enough. Yes, you were in a bad situation for a period of time but you **survived**. You were strong enough to cope as it happened and you were strong enough to say you are ready to get help and begin healing just by virtue of having opened this book and reading as far as you have. That deserves celebrating as you work through healing.

Grieve Properly

Grief is absolutely expected when someone dies, or a relationship ends for one reason or another. We all go through grief at different periods of time and for different reasons. One most people do not have to go through, however, grieving the persona the narcissist used to win you over or grieve the relationship you should have had with a family member. You cared deeply for the persona that was snuffed out like a candle with no trace of it remaining. It is normal to feel a deep sense of loss for the person you loved. Likewise, if the narcissist in your life is a parent, grandparent or other family members, it is normal to grieve that relationship and the fact that you did not get the parent or grandparent that every child deserves. Grieving this relationship is one of the steps toward healing from the loss.

Like healing from an injury, grief comes in multiple stages. Typically, five are recognized: The grieving individual will begin in denial, move on to anger, then bargaining, followed by depression and finally, he will reach acceptance for the situation. Remember, grief comes and goes in waves, and there is no true end to it. It will continue to happen throughout your life, though it grows easier to cope with as time goes by. In the beginning, it is raw and frequent, but you will find the frequency declining over time.

Release Negative Feelings

As a primary target for a narcissist, you are likely empathetic to some degree. As an empath, you likely have a propensity to absorb the emotions of those around you. You may have internalized some of the narcissist's own negativity because of the exposure to them. You may see some of the narcissist's negative traits in you, such as realizing that you are snapping at people the same way he snapped at you or that you have been thinking about yourself in the way that the narcissist thought of himself. You might feel uncharacteristically angry at the world.

No matter the negative feelings, you need to develop an outlet for them.

If left alone, you may feel as though your very self is festering within you, as though the toxicity from the narcissist still threatens to overwhelm you and turn you into someone you know you are not. The solution to this is to find a good outlet for yourself. Some people pour themselves into a creative hobby, such as drawing, writing, painting, music, dance, or any other form of creating something else. They literally channel their feelings into their art, allowing the negativity to flow through them and out into the world so it can no longer consume them. Others choose physical exercise as an outlet, choosing to sweat out the negativity with each rep of the weight set, or with each mile run. Others still may decide to nurture something else, such as growing and tending to a garden, bringing back those tender feelings that were once familiar to them. No matter what you choose as your healthy outlet, what is important is that you feel better after engaging in it, and that you see that your general outlook and mood is improving the more you do it. Anything is acceptable here so long as it allows you to channel your negativity in a way that works for you and that you enjoy.

Create a Support Network

As in all great endeavors, a support network is crucial. These are people you can fall back on for advice, support, or even just a quiet ear to listen in tough times. Being able to speak to other people who truly understand your struggles, your journey, and what you have gone through is incredibly validating. You feel understood and legitimized and you find other people who have been in your shoes who may be further down the route to healing than you are. These are people who will not try to pick apart your experiences or try to sidestep the issues you are dealing with. They understand what it means to be vulnerable to a narcissist and having them on your side will provide clearer insight for you.

Through the internet, you may also find support groups specific to the narcissistic relationship you found yourself in. With a few specific web searches, you can locate an online community for narcissistic romantic partners.

Support networks imply that you will be opening up to others about the abuse you endured in person, face to face with others. Some people are not comfortable with this idea but luckily, the internet has made finding groups of people like you easier than ever before.

Self-Care

Self-care is crucial in the period of healing. After spending so long under the narcissist's thumb and catering to him, you may find your own wellbeing quite neglected. Despite what the narcissist may have convinced you of, you deserve self-care. What better time than now to start investing in your hobbies or taking time to relax? You can take yourself on a solo date to a movie and dinner with your own company or read that new book you had been dying to finish. By beginning to care for yourself, you will begin to feel like the true you that you knew prior to the narcissist wreaking havoc in your life.

Self-care will be crucial for yourself as you heal. You have spent so long catering to others, namely the narcissist, and now you deserve some pampering of your own. You deserve to go the extra mile for yourself, to treat yourself and remind yourself that you truly appreciate the person that you are, recognizing that you have one life with one body, and that you should appreciate what you have. Take this time to spend some extra money on some bath bombs, if that is your thing, and take a long, warm bath to soak and relax. You could even bring yourself a book and a glass of wine to enjoy as you soaked if you enjoy wine and reading. You could spend the money to get yourself a gym membership to exercise and work on your stamina. You could decide to take a cooking class and learn to make a few new dishes for yourself now that you have the time. Anything that you have ever wanted to do goes here, so long as it is constructive and helps you feel more at ease.

When you care for yourself, you should make sure you are nourishing both your body and mind. Take care of yourself the way you would take care of your child, and your body will thank you for it. Spend time every day engaging in some level of self-care, whether it is waking up an hour earlier before work to go on a walk at dawn or signing yourself up for a few classes in the evenings to finally learn those new skills. No matter what you choose, make sure you dedicate plenty of time to caring for yourself, as that level of self-care will eventually become your habitual default, and you will find yourself feeling far more well rested. By caring for yourself now, you will allow yourself to heal from the narcissist's abuse and begin to flourish into who you would have been without the narcissist's influence. You will begin to feel like yourself again.

Self-Reflect

Your method for self-reflection can be anything from journaling to inner-monologues in which you explore why you were so tolerant of the abuse. Start by taking a few moments to find a quiet location and relax. You will then begin by thinking about whatever you will reflect on; perhaps your narcissist's abuse. Consider how you felt about the abuse, and write down every thought that comes to mind, a stream of consciousness style. This lets you get everything out in the open all at once, and even if you feel the need to cry, scream, or like you do not want to keep going because it is too painful, push through anyway. This is an important step to understanding what was going on in your own mind during the time. The goal here is to identify everything you can about the topic, in this case, the narcissist's abusive tendencies. If you felt scared, write that down. Angry? Write that down, too. Anything is valid. After a short period of time, stop writing and put your journal away. You can return to it later.

Either that night or the next day, after you have had the chance to calm down, revisit your writing for the day from an impartial lens. You want to begin to analyze your pattern of thoughts so you can identify what it was about the narcissist that was worth putting up with his treatment of you.

Start Therapy

Perhaps the most obvious step, seeking therapy is incredibly beneficial to people who have been through trauma. This can teach you how to cope with what you have been through and provide you with methods to stay strong. It also can help you identify the reasons you were seen as an easy victim, to begin with, and aid in remedying that. Very few people in this world would not benefit from therapy or counseling, so do not feel as if you should be ashamed for needing it. There is nothing wrong with getting extra support for a serious problem, and being abused would definitely classify as a traumatic or serious problem.

CBT is one of the more common and quick methods used for learning to restructure thoughts and become less vulnerable to abuse and deception in the future. If you have a self-confidence problem, CBT can teach you to become more confident and that you are deserving of the same respect and consideration others demand. If it is due to a disordered vision of what love is, CBT can help you override your misconceptions and help you learn what a healthy relationship looks like. No matter what the issue is, this therapy will be prepared to help you. If you are unsure of where to start, speak to your primary care doctor. They can start a referral to therapists in your area and give you a general starting point.

Trauma, especially from abuse from someone you loved and trusted, can be quite damaging to a person. You may feel as though you struggle to cope at times, or that some of your insecurities that the narcissist has installed are so deeply ingrained that you will never be able to get out from underneath them. Maybe you have no clear idea of where to go with your healing and you feel like you need guidance. No matter what, whether you are coping with your abuse better or worse than average, you could benefit from seeking therapy.

Nearly every single person in this world would benefit from therapy in some form. Therapy teaches us how to better solve problems, how to cope with negativity, how to think, and sometimes just helps unpack difficult, traumatic events.

Affirmations

Affirmations have three important features: they need to be positive, about yourself and present tense. So long as whatever you create meets those three standards, it has the CBT seal of approval. It is important for the affirmation to be positive because that will keep your mindset healthy and positive. It is hard to think in positives when you tell yourself "I will never tell myself I am unworthy," as opposed to, "I am worthy of the respect I demand, and I will treat myself as such." The first sentence is a negative frame of mind, and despite the fact that it has a generally positive meaning, it is still worded in such a way that you will continue to think in negatives. By rewording it to be positive, you shift your mindset to a healthier one. The affirmation must be about yourself because ultimately, the only thing in the world you have control over is yourself. You can influence other things, but the only thing entirely within your control is you. If your affirmation focuses on someone else, you have no way to make it true, no matter how much you tell it to yourself. Lastly, keeping the affirmation in the present tense means it is currently true when you say it. Since these are said in moments of self-doubt or weakness, saying that you are currently worthy of respect or to be loved keeps you strong because you are reminding yourself it is currently true at that particular moment.

When you develop affirmations and use them regularly, you can recite them to help yourself begin shifting your own negative thoughts into ones that are far more productive.

Chapter 4: Healing After Emotional or Psychological Abuse

Dealing with Emotional Abuse

The problem with emotional abuse is that the person who is being abused is often clueless that it is happening. That all comes down to gas lighting, and the fact that the narcissist has used is to so slowly and subtly, that it has crept up on them without them even noticing it. By the time they start to question what is really happening, and perhaps someone else makes them aware of it, getting out of the situation has become very difficult indeed.

Emotional abuse often flies under the radar and isn't given the same amount of shock factor as those who are victims of physical abuse. This is probably because there are no physical scars to see; you can't see the scars that someone inflicts emotionally, they can only be felt. The thing is, physical abuse heals, and whilst it certainly leaves mental scars, finding support is usually an easier process. Society has made it far more difficult to seek help for emotional issues; we tend to recognize what we can see. Hopefully, in the future, that will change, but the tides are turning and there is a lot more recognition of emotional abuse as a damaging factor than ever before.

Over time, emotional abuse can cause a person to question their entire sanity, making them live with cripplingly low self-worth and self-confidence. They will become house-bound, alienating themselves from those close to them and avoiding anything socially minded. This is not a happy or healthy life.

The following steps will help you deal with the emotional abuse that a narcissistic relationship may be throwing your way.

- Identify What is Really Happening - First things first, you need to be honest with yourself and see things for what they truly are; you are being emotionally abused by a narcissist. Yes, you may love this person, but this relationship is not healthy for you, and you are the main concern here, right now.

- Make Your Own Health a Priority - Your mental and physical health should be the most important thing on your mind right now. Stop trying to please your partner, and instead turn your attention inwards. Make steps towards increasing your confidence, perhaps by finding a new hobby or starting the gym and boosting your health and confidence. Practice self-care and allow yourself to heal, before making positive, affirmative steps.

- Set Yourself Boundaries - It's vital that you set boundaries with your partner. Tell them that they cannot shout at you like that, they can't insult you, they can't call you names. You should also tell them that if they continue to do this, you will leave. If they do it again, simply walk out of the room. It's vital that you follow through on these boundaries.

- Stop the Blame Game - Anyone who has been subject to emotional abuse at the hands of a narcissist will probably send a large proportion of their day blaming themselves for everything that goes wrong in the relationship. This needs to stop. Ask yourself this very painful, but very real question - why would someone who claims to love you act this way? Yes, they have a condition, but does this mean you have to suffer? No. You cannot control the situation, so avoid blaming yourself for it.

- Be Very Clear in Your Own Mind That You Cannot Fix Them - Do your research into NPD and be very clear that you cannot fix them, so don't even try. You can attempt to have a conversation with them and perhaps highlight the fact that you suspect they may have NPD, but a true narcissist is probably going to throw that idea right out of the window and blame you for suggesting it. You're going around in circles and it's time to break the chain.

- Build up a Network of Support - Confide in someone you trust about the reality of your situation and do not feel ashamed or guilty about it. The more support you can muster, and it is out there, the easier it will be for you to gain perspective and become strong enough to make your final step.

- Walk Away - Sounds easy, but it's not in practice. Put together a plan which allows you to walk away from this abusive relationship with your head held high. Know in your heart that your partner will try to pull you back, but that is the whole point of putting together the support network we mentioned in our last step. Be strong and know that you do not deserve to be abused, by someone who has a condition or otherwise.

- Seek Help if You Need it - It's not a weakness to ask for help, and if after you've finally broken the relationship you need to speak to a professional in order to work through the issues you've faced, then do it. Most people who have been in these types of relationships do need some kind of therapy or counseling afterwards, in order to build their self-confidence and sense of self-worth once more. By doing this, you're investing in your future, when you meet someone who truly does deserve your kind heart.

Indications That you are Recovering from Narcissistic Trauma and Abuse

- You realize and understand that self-care is an everyday priority - This first sign is that you have finally come to the acceptance that when you put yourself first, you are making steps forward. Self-care is perhaps the utmost importance in recovering from your past trauma and abuse. Self-care may include things like saying no more often, taking a nap when you feel overwhelmed or tired, eating healthier, exercising daily, creating boundaries, and making wiser decisions.

- You do everything you have to, to protect your physical and mental well-being - You notice the identity of a narcissist, and you realize that their feelings were never real. You understand the pain you went through, or are going through currently, and have vowed to not let it happen again.

- You don't care about what your ex thinks. - Remember the time where you were sitting there, after your separation, and you wondered if they were thinking about you, what they were doing, and how they were living their lives without you.

- You are more focused on your own life than what your ex is doing with theirs. - Because you know that if you go back to your ex, you will only be living with the repeated abuse that you experienced before, you no longer care to be engaged with them. You are at a state where you have worked really hard to get where you are now and realize that the most important thing is to take care of yourself.

- You come up with solutions, rather than focus on your problems. - You have come to a realization that you have the power, and strength to change your circumstances. You have accepted that control, and power is in your hands, and not theirs.

- You see the past abuse as an opportunity, rather than a punishment like you once had. - Regardless if your low self-esteem or unconfident behaviors were stemmed from your childhood, or not, you now realize that going through the relationship of a narcissist was an opportunity to overcome these weaknesses.

Taking Some Time to Your Sense of Self

When you were in the abusive relationship, it is likely that you spent a lot of your time doing things that the narcissist wanted. You would make sure that all of their needs were met, and that they would be happy with you. Of course, the narcissist was never happy with anything that you tried to give to them, and this caused you to give up more and more of your time, and more and more of yourself, in the process. By the time the narcissist is done with you, or you are able to escape from the abuse, you are likely to have very little idea of your own self and even the things that you like and don't like.

The sooner that you are able to develop your own sense of self after the abuse, the better off that you will be. Knowing your own sense of self will allow you to see the narcissist for who they are. It allows you to start valuing yourself again and you will gain the self-esteem and self-confidence that is needed. You will know your strengths and appreciate your weaknesses, and then you will work to keep these at the forefront. When you know your sense of self, you are less likely to sit at home pining after the narcissist and letting them take the control over you that they want.

This is going to be hard. The narcissist spent a lot of time working to take away your sense of self. When you have no sense of self, then you are mare likely to just go along with whatever the narcissist would like. Developing this is so important so that you can move on from your life and never go back to the narcissist. There are a number of things that you can do after leaving an abusive relationship to gain your sense of self back again, and some of the best options to include in this discovery includes:

Eating well

When the relationship is ending with a narcissist, it is important for you to learn how to eat healthy. Whether or not you did this before your relationship was over is not going to matter. You need to make sure that you keep up a healthy diet because it is going to do wonders when it comes to your overall health and how well you are able to heal after the abuse is done.

Eating healthy foods will make a world of difference in how well you are going to feel. While it is fine to indulge yourself a bit on occasion, it is best if you are able to stick with a generally healthy diet plan. Eating lots of fresh and wholesome foods will help you to feel so much better than ever before, and will ensure that you actually give your body, and your whole mind, the care that they need.

Exercise

Rather than sitting at home and doing nothing, making it easier for the narcissist to get back into your life, you may find that getting out of the house and exercise, whether you go on a walk or go to a class. This frees up your mind, helps you to actually be a bit social, and makes the narcissist the furthest thing from your mind. The endorphins that are going to be released in the brain during exercise can lift up feelings of depression, can help you to improve your self-esteem, and can generally make you feel better about yourself, much better than every before. Even twenty minutes of working out each day will make a big difference. When you add in a good exercise program to your routine, you are going to see some positive changes in your physique, and that is going to make you feel self-confident and increase your self-esteem.

Start a new hobby

Sometimes working on a new hobby is the perfect way to find your old sense of self. Taking some time each day, or when you are able, to work on something that is fun, or that is just yours, where there aren't any expectations or obligations that you need to meet, an make a world of difference when you are recovering from a narcissistic relationship. The hobby can be anything that you would like. Maybe you decide to start painting, to write in a journal or write a story, go for a walk, spend time with friends, learn how to cook and more.

Spend time with friends and family

Now that the relationship is over, it is time to get back some of those relationships. Depending on how long the abuse went on and how bad the situation got, you may find that some of your friends and some of your family members are still hurt about the experience, and they will not want to have anything to do with you now. You have to accept that. Maybe at some other point, when they see that you are really done with the situation and ready to move on, they will come back. But you have to realize that they were harmed in this too and they may not be willing to forgive.

Be open to new experiences

This is the perfect chance to figure out the true sense of self that is hidden inside. It is likely that you may not like some of the experiences, but then some may surprise you, and some you are going to like quite a bit. This is a learning experience and the more things that you get out there and do, the more that you are going to learn about the true you that is there.

If someone asks you to come along and try something, then go ahead and do it. If you see that there is a class going on in your town and you want to do that as well, then try it out. If there is something that you have always wanted to do or learn or try, then this is the perfect chance for you to get started.

Find your sense of self

One of the things that you need to concentrate on when it comes to healing after the abusive relationship is that you need to take some time to find yourself. This can be hard. Even after you have stopped talking or doing anything with the narcissist, some of their words are still going to ring through your head. You still believe that you are not worth their time and attention. You may not believe that you have a true self separated from the narcissist.

Now that the relationship is over with the narcissist, it is time to start focusing on yourself again. This can be hard for a victim to do because they have spent so much time hearing that they were not worth attention, that their strengths were weaknesses, and that they were the one to blame for everything that went wrong in the relationship, while the narcissist was the one to blame for all of the good stuff that happened.

This is going to be a process, one that takes a lot of time and effort in order to accomplish. but if you are willing to take your time, to let the control of the narcissist leave you, and really enjoy the new life that you are creating by following the steps above, you are going to be able to find your own sense of self in no time.

The power of self healing

I believe strongly in the power of self-healing, and I believe that any degree of emotional pain can be addressed through self-care and healing practices over time. It may be a long road and will certainly not be easy, but with proper support and belief in yourself, it is possible to move past the experience of narcissistic abuse to a large degree. You may not be able to erase the effects entirely, but it is possible to move and live a healthy, productive, and emotionally stable life after even the most damaging of emotional experiences. This is because the human brain has an incredible capacity to rewire itself and relearn how to live and love through healthy habits and new thought cycles that will take the place of the old, destructive thought cycles.

First of all, grab an old journal or buy yourself a nice new one. Many survivors of abuse can attest to the power of simply writing out and processing your feelings through words. There may be many aspects of your experience with narcissistic abuse that you have yet to really address or wrap your mind around. Write about how this made you feel, then reinforce the fact that there is nothing wrong with your body and that this was just one of many tools your abuser used to break you down. Replace these negative thoughts with positive, affirming thoughts about your beautiful body and what it has done for you. Expressions of gratitude can also go a long way to dispel feelings of worthlessness and emptiness.

Educating yourself about narcissists and their tactics is going to be very important as you want to arm yourself against future abusers. If you feel you were too quick to trust in your last relationship, you may need to practice setting up barriers and waiting for people to prove to you that they are trustworthy.

Meditation can be a very helpful tool throughout this process. Begin by sitting comfortably in a space that is quiet and free of distraction. Practice breathing slowly and taking deep breaths each time you breathe in. Focus on your body in space and feel each part of your body as you breathe. There are several guided meditations available online for you to peruse if you so desire, or you may choose to come up with your own little mantra. Whatever you decide to do, try to make some time each and every day to focus in on your affirmation. Repeat the words to yourself slowly, over and over. Tell yourself that you love yourself, that you forgive yourself, that you are enough, that you are loved, that you are strong.

Finally, do what you can to cultivate a regular sleep schedule where you get at least 8 hours of sleep. Setting aside some time at night before bedtime for meditation may be a great way to help your brain settle down and prepare for rest. Try to go to bed at the same time every night and do something calming right before. Try not to eat and snack on junk food late at night as this will keep you up longer and may disrupt your sleep.

Know that you are strong enough to move past this horrific ordeal and that you are not alone in your experience. Relearn to love and take care of yourself and reaffirm each day that you are worth the effort of recovery.

Steel yourself should your abuser ever re-enter your life for any reason. Enforce strict boundaries and enforce a rule of no contact whatsoever. Do not answer phone calls, texts, anything. He is not worth it, and there is nothing positive that he can offer you. You have risen above that influence.

Overcoming Loneliness After Narcissistic Abuse

Although being with a narcissist is a truly horrific and often traumatic experience, breaking free can lead to initial loneliness. You are so used to being with that person, being involved in their stories, games, and sense of companionship even if it is a twisted and mentally-emotionally abusive companionship; that finally leaving and being free can leave you feeling empty.

Connected to this is a self-recovery, healing and boundary plan. Boundaries are very important, but so is your personal re-discovery of self and self-healing. Below are the key and highly effective ways to overcome loneliness.

Passion Projects

Immerse yourself in a passion project. New hobbies, favorite pastimes or creating a vision board to align with your dreams and aspirations can all be marvelous gateways back to your true self. Following your greatest joy allows you to overcome loneliness and heal from the sufferings caused by your narcissistic partner. Passion and fire are the spark of life, they re-energize and revitalize your inner core further enabling you to stop feeling isolated or cut off from the world. This is an unfortunate consequence of being the victim of narcissistic abuse or mind manipulations-you may feel disconnected to others on a profound level. Refinding yourself through a passion project is essential for your wellbeing.

Re-finding Yourself This is knowing yourself on every level; your intentions, goals, dreams, hidden motivations and your personality in its entirety. We usually become lost and allow in the illusions and judgments of others when we do not know ourselves. 'The self' is the holistic part of being, the persona, characteristics and beliefs which make us unique. It is our thoughts, feelings, subtle impressions, emotions, past experience and deeper inner workings, also having a soulful aspect or significance. Recovering from a narcissist and re-finding yourself tie in closely to knowing yourself, or knowing thyself. Not only can taking steps to rediscover and know thyself help you overcome loneliness, it will also help increase your self-esteem, self-worth and personal confidence.

New Social Groups and Organizations

Balanced with all the other key ways to overcome loneliness and heal for the long term is the engagement of new social groups and organizations. This can include peer support, groups for victims of narcissistic abuse, or simply any organization or venture which allows you to feel good. Being happy and connecting with others is the best way to let go and move forward with your life, despite the initial loneliness you may feel. You can feel lonely or isolated in a group too as the truth is-loneliness is just a mindset. Some people feel lonely even when surrounded by family and peers, just as many feel most at peace and blissful when alone. True happiness and contentment comes from your ability to connect and feel at ease with the world. Taking the first steps by putting yourself out there will re-spark your passion for life and connection, and your connection with yourself.

Strengthen your Emotional Muscles

Strengthening and developing your emotional muscles must be part of your boundary plan. Your emotional resilience, intelligence and connection are your keys to success. Empathy, intuition and an advanced to mature emotional connection to both yourself and others (the world around) allows you to stay centered within and aligned to your truth, own reality and choice to stay clear from narcissistic abuse, and the games of your ex. Emotions can be seen as a muscle, even if figuratively as they control and shape all of physical reality as we know it.

How to Trust Others and Yourself Again

Now that the relationship is over, part of what you feel may be just the fact that you can never trust someone else again due to the betrayal and hurt you went through. If you let yourself stay in this dark place, without opening your mind to the possibility that not all people are like that, then you will stay unpleasant and become bitter.

Reclaiming Your Reality

Forgive yourself and seek reminders of who you are. This is another time-consuming process, and should never be rushed. Don't allow so-called friends and family members guilt you into "getting over it"; this is especially true for men recovering from abuse. Take as much time as you need and tell those who would push too hard to take a hike. This is an important first step in recovering **yourself**. You were a strong, capable person once, and you will be again. The first thing you need to do is treat yourself with respect, and demand that others in your close circles do, too.

Rebuilding Your Trust

When dealing with people in your various friendships and acquaintances, give people the opportunity to show their intention. Call them on it. Ask them about their intentions. You can do this neutrally, even in a friendly tone—this is not a call to arms and you never need to sound combative. Being assertive and seeing with both eyes open is a healthy way of dealing with other people. Don't be afraid to take the initiative.

Listen to your intuitive instincts

Intuition is when your body gives you warning signs when something is wrong, or when you should be cautious before proceeding. Intuition can come in forms of racing thoughts right before you are about to do something, a feeling that you should run or freeze, or a vibe like chills or hairs standing up on your neck. Maybe a chill rush down your spine. Have you ever done something dangerous, or been in the line-up to a rollercoaster ride? That feeling you get as you step closer to the ride; your body and mind may be screaming at you not to go through with this. Or maybe your first kiss or date with someone you just met, that feeling you get right before your lips meet, or the feeling you have when you're sitting across a table from them on your date. This is your intuition. Sometimes your instincts scream at you to continue going, and other times, it tells you no. Learning to listen to it takes practice and life experience as you go through the roles of the ups and downs. Can you remember what you felt the minute you met your last girlfriend or boyfriend? The first impression is a judgment we make, usually right after our intuition speaks to us.

Mistakes to avoid during the Recovery Process

Escaping narcissistic abuse is not easy; in fact, it may be one of the toughest things you can break free of. With their control, extremely impressive manipulative ways, and hoovering techniques, you may find yourself going back to them more than you want or staying in the relationship longer than you should.

Believing that researching more about narcissists will make you better - This belief stops you from moving forward because it triggers the abuse that you just went through, thus stopping your process from succeeding. This is because the rational and logical analyzing part of your brain has no direct access or contact with the emotional part of your brain - I like to call it the wise mind, vs. the emotional mind.

Assigning blame - We should not blame ourselves, but just accept that most of our actions were a cause from ourselves. We got into the relationship, and we stayed longer than we should have. We are in charge of our decisions, and whether or not we made the right or wrong choices, we learned from them. The main reason we blame others for providing or not providing for us what we need is because we haven't yet learned to provide it for ourselves, which gives us codependency and the habits of being with people that seek out our weaknesses for exploitation purposes.

Replacing the love of another with the love of someone else - Most people would call this a "rebound," in which case it is. We want the love and attention of someone else, because we were so badly hurt by our narcissistic spouse or loved one. One of the problems that could happen with this type of behavior is that when you try to replace your narcissist partner, you may come up short, which then makes you crave the attention of the narcissist even more.

Unrealistic expectations of the amount of time needed to recover - Because of the feelings that we want to be loved, held, and noticed, we often try to rush the recovery and healing stages. Just when we start to feel better, we may think that it's all done, and then jump into something else faster than we should. When we expect the process to take a certain amount of time, we set ourselves up for failure.

Chapter 5: Disarming the narcissist

Feed their ego

A narcissist needs a lot of attention, affection, praise, and adoration to thrive. So, by complimenting him and feeding his fragile ego, you can easily handle living with a narcissist. You must be prepared to keep feeding his ego, if not, be prepared to deal with his tantrums. This is something you will need to get used to if leaving the narcissist is not an option for you. A couple of simple compliments can go a long way while trying to deal with a narcissist. This is not manipulation. Instead, it is about understanding his personality disorder and using it to help smooth things out.

With narcissists, it is very easy for us to shift our focus onto them, mainly because we often we feel like we have no choice and as if we are being forced into those frustrating interactions with them. There is no way of navigating our own feelings and emotions when a narcissist is around because they are so vindictive and demanding of our undivided attention that it becomes increasingly more difficult for us to function at a normal, clear-minded level. We find this mentally destabilizing and the hardest part about interactions with a narcissist is the normalization period after where we sit in utter bewilderment, struggling to comprehend how such a person can take such a mental toll on our minds.

Narcissism - or rather **people** who have Narcissistic Personality Disorder – is not just a personality disorder. It is an array of traits and characteristics in which congregate and formulate within someone's **identity.** A narcissist's identity is an infliction in itself. They have a heightened sense of identity, meaning that they are individuals who only see the best in themselves, although exaggeratedly, and cannot see their own faults and flaws. Like with Narcissus, his successors only see their best reflection, one that only reflects positivity, beauty, and success, and this develops, in their minds at least, that they deserve recognition from us for all of that. They embody an unnatural yet common persona of "gods amongst men". And this, though buried deep within a narcissist is a sensitive being, affects us – people who are not narcissists – even more. A narcissist's words and way of exuberant bragging degrade us and that degradation is unhealthy for us. It breeds self-doubt, it impairs our ability to succeed because we believe the judgment of someone who themselves cannot stand – or even believe – judgment. They are critical of us and we need to learn how to deal with them.

Let us go back to that word. **Sensitive.** Narcissists are sensitive individuals who lack empathy and outward emotion towards others, yet possess such a deep and in-tune emotional connection with themselves. This makes them highly oblivious to their own faults and flaws which, in turn, when pointed out to them, they simply cannot believe you. So creates a grudge which can often linger for months to years to a lifetime. Narcissists are, staying with sensitivity, incredibly reactive to rejection. This could be towards how they look, what they do for a living, what they have said, and their opinion. Remember, a narcissist is "always right" and for you to challenge that stance often has a more hurtful outcome for you. Why? Because we cannot win against or challenge a narcissist and that is something we must deal with.

However, with this said, do not make promises with a narcissist. To rephrase that – do not allow yourself to believe that a promise made by a narcissist will be seen through and kept. Though a narcissist will never forget a grudge or a person who "once said something about me", they will almost always "forget" a promise made. A reason for this could be that we have already given the narcissist what they want and they have simply **moved on.** The best piece of advice for this, if a narcissist has made a promise with you, is to be persistent in order to make sure that their word is kept. Yes, in a way, this is challenging the narcissist, though this route is not challenging their credibility.

Dealing with narcissists is something we have all done and gone through and through those interactions we know now that dealing with narcissists is like dealing with a hostage situation; something can always go wrong and we will feel the effects of that for a very long, long time. Narcissists have this austere and gravitas about them that sometimes, when dealing with relationships, can come across as them being charismatic, which at first is true. However, this is an effect of them being the one in control of every possible outlet and outcome of the relationship through their campaign of strong manipulation. How can we tell when they are manipulating us? Assess the situation as a politician would when dealing with a conflict resolution crisis in some foreign country-look at the situation, how it has benefited you, the narcissist, and then see who it really has benefitted. The answer will often shock you.

With a narcissist, think of them as the driver of the fancy car with you next to them in some dingy wagon, even if you both drive the same car – such is the gravitational pull to their perfect selves and lives that they will idealize themselves, congratulate themselves, shower themselves with praise and adulation, and try to outdo whatever it is that you have ever accomplished. The point being: we will always be a backseat passenger when it comes to our friendships, relationships, and associations with a narcissist, never at the wheel or beside them.

We need to accept that there simply is no win-win outcome with a narcissist.

But how can we deal with them? There are three main ways of dealing with a narcissist – **acknowledgment** and **understanding.** There are other methods that we could use that would be beneficial to us when dealing with a narcissist, such as staying calm, relaxation, channeling the narcissist out, or deeper psychological methods (when in a toxic relationship with one) such as therapy and meditation.

Acknowledgment

When we are dealing with a narcissist whose opinion seems to be the only one that "should be taken into account" we can simply acknowledge the narcissist, thank them for their opinion, and then to make sure that we have made certain that they seem sure that we appreciate their opinion. We can thank them and do whatever we want with that information. By acknowledging the narcissist's opinion we have navigated a safer route around the definite feeling of scorn that would have otherwise been directed towards us by the narcissist. By doing this we have been the "adult" in the situation and have seemingly heightened the narcissist's self-esteem by making them think that we *will* use their advice and suggestions, even though to a degree we will not be taking it into consideration. Avoiding the conflict which comes from challenging the narcissist's opinion allows us to show an interest in what the narcissist has said.

Understanding

Though acknowledging a narcissist implies that we *listen* and do not take into consideration, understanding the narcissist is by actually *listening* to them and taking into account what they have said is a little bit more complex. Though this tactic can usually save us from the wrath of the narcissist, understanding their opinion takes a little more nous. We need to make sure that we let them know that we value them and then listen to what they have said, keenly listening until, from underneath all that self-absorbed theory, we can piece together our own picture of what they have said. This can be entirely frustrating but it is something that sometimes we should do. Behind their mask is someone who has gotten to the top quickly, despite stepping on everyone to get there. Often, when we dissect what they have said and omitted the **spotlight fever** connotations we can actually get a clear picture of what they are talking about, thus meaning that the advice they have given can actually be applied to a certain situation in which we are going through.

Staying Calm

If you are not a person who can easily deal with a narcissist then staying calm is by far the most difficult practice for you when they start going on about this and that. It irks you, creates this massive bubble of steaming water that wants to spill over. We all have been there, don't worry. It is that feeling when what they have said is so mean or just dumbfounded that we ball up our fists, sigh, smile, and nod our heads; that frustration that is about to explode; the emotion of complete and utter anger that fills us and consumes us. But we can deal with that emotion. It takes time to perfect it but staying calm, especially when the narcissist you are around is persistent in his or her presentation of themselves, can be a life-changing tool in being at peace with the situation or interaction. Sure, it is extremely difficult but acceptance of that situation or interaction with the narcissist and then finding a small piece of calm within you can certainly go a long way. For instance, a narcissist starts explaining all that you did wrong, whether this narcissist is someone at work or your loved one, and you become awash with anger but know how the narcissist will react, do you shout and go off and get nowhere with the narcissist or do you try your best to stay calm, listen, and then just move on? Everybody snaps eventually and that is our human nature, our survival instincts kicking in. It is a normal reaction. It is the pressure building up and our tempers becoming unhinged. But, we do need to be aware that by arguing with or retorting back at a narcissist only affects you and not them.

Channeling the Narcissist Out

This is the opposite of acknowledging and understanding a narcissist. channeling out the narcissist is the basic term for *I do not want to be around you because you make me feel worthless for your own personal gain.* Another way of saying this could be that you have taken the decision to cut out the narcissist in your life who has had a negative impact on you mentally and physically. Although, yes, the attachment to them is quite strong and the process will be difficult, the step forward for you will have such positive effects on your life. However, channeling out a narcissist can also be someone at work who you have chosen not to listen to because of their self-centered nature. This could have a big impact on your work life, whereas before you had to deal with the feeling of doubt and hurt, you can now flourish in an environment where you are more comfortable, at peace, and at ease without the mental strain of being around the narcissist.

When you first begin to realize that you're with someone who's a narcissist, it can be devastating. You may spend more time agonizing over the fact that you fell for your partner's act than even trying to figure out how to get back on your feet. "How did I let this happen to me?" you might ask yourself. The first thing to understand is that the fault is not yours to claim: it belongs solely in the lap of the narcissist. The only mistakes you made were believing that people were capable of love, which they still are. You fell victim to a master mimic and manipulator.

Defend the Borders

Remember that you have the right to say no. It's your body, your heart, your mind. If any of your rights are being violated, say so, neutrally and assertively. If your words are ignored, have consequences ready in place to be invoked. Consequences are not punishments (although your abuser may say otherwise); they are meant to protect you from being harmed any further. If you must leave to go to a friend's house, calmly explain why. When you return, reiterate why you chose to leave if the narcissist brings it up.

Living with a narcissist or implementing a real relationship with a darker personality disorder person can leave you second guessing everything. This is because you no longer trust yourself or others around you and is why it is so crucial to heal through personal growth, to get past this. The biggest reasons why trust seems so difficult after a narcissistic relationship is because you are fearful that it will happen again, being alone has now become very new, and new things can be scary, and the narcissist has damaged your perception of life, and so you see everyone as a narcissist. If trust already doesn't come easy to you, then learning to trust again, may be even more difficult.

Chapter 6: Dealing with Anger

Anger occurs after discovering that the narcissist, the person you thought you knew and loved, was a lie and an act. At the bargaining stage, you tell yourself and the narcissist that the relationship can continue if certain things happen. You may believe that your narcissistic partner will have fewer issues if you give him more attention or affection. You try to tell yourself that the relationship is salvageable if you continue to make sacrifices and that the persona you fell in love with will come back if you do everything perfectly. In the end, you feel as though continued sacrifices, no matter how miserable they make you, would be better than losing your loved one. Soon, depression sets in as you realize the futility of everything. You cannot bring back the persona you thought existed, and you lose hope.

While caring for yourself, look for ways to release your anger, fear or other negative feelings you have built up during your relationship. Empaths, who are some of the narcissists' favorite people to target, absorb the feelings of those around them. They begin to take on the other people's feelings, and when surrounded by a narcissist, those emotions are largely toxic. You need to release this pent up anger you have internalized in order to begin to heal truly. Just like cleaning a physical wound is crucial to healing correctly, you must also take care to clean your mental wounds as well.

Despite the fact that your relationship with the narcissist took a turn toward abusive, you still likely developed real, strong feelings for her. You loved her, or rather, the idea of her that she originally presented to you when attempting the love bombing stage, when she mirrored your heart's desires. You fell in love with an idea, which quickly was obliterated by the narcissist that was left behind, staring back at you with the face of the one you loved, as if your loved one had suddenly become possessed. You deserve the chance to grieve that relationship. Though the person that you loved was never a real person, she was real to you, and because of that, you should allow yourself to grieve the anger out. If not for the person you lost, then grieve for not getting the relationship you deserved when you fell in love with the narcissist.

Admit the pain, or anger

- Vent, and let it out to the people who are most supportive - or write about it.
- Determine your response to your emotions (are you going to sit here and feel sorry for yourself, or are you going to try to get up and take care of yourself today?)
- Stick to your goals, and your plan to recovering and making it through this first stage of devastation

- Forget it. Shift your thoughts to something else, something more positive. You can only learn to forget once the other steps are taken care of.

Anger will destroy your sense of accomplishment and hold you from doing things you used to enjoy. This stage in the process is to fight back - do the opposite of what you feel. So, if you feel like sitting in bed all day, get up and sit on the couch, or outside for the day. Distract your mind with telephone calls to loved ones, play crosswords, exercise, write, draw, **etc.** Do something creative, and don't allow yourself to sit with this pain.

Whatever your routine was before, continue with it. If it is hard to fully maintain a routine right now, just do a couple a day, then gradually increase your strength to move on to the next thing you used to do.

Find a place that doesn't trigger you.

If your breakup consisted of them moving, and you are stuck with all the memories no matter where you look, consider moving or staying with a friend for a while. If you had to move, and it hurts to go out and see the places you guys walked or went on dates, avoid these places, and find somewhere new to go. Just don't avoid it forever.

Give in to the need for closeness - without sexual contact. The fastest way to get through this stage is physical closeness. So, if you have a child, cuddle them, if you have a best friend, ask for lots of hugs. When you need a shoulder to cry on, reach out to someone you trust. Along with this physical closeness, bonding with people you trust is a bonus in this recovery.

Allow Yourself to Grieve

Believe it or not, crying, and tears are beneficial to your recovery. Crying is scientifically proven to rid your body of stress. When you let your other emotions in, this also helps with the grieving process. However, if you hold your emotions in, you are making connections in your brain that suggests holding it in is a better solution and will actually cause more problems for you later. When people hold their tears, and anger in, they never learn to release or let go. Instead they teach themselves that it is okay to hold it in, which can result in an outburst later. Have you ever cried so hard, then after you get this foggy feeling, but it feels as though a weight has almost lifted? This is because you have relieved yourself of the tension or stress that you feel.

Staying Calm

If you are not a person who can easily deal with a narcissist, then staying calm is by far the most difficult practice for you when they start going on about this and that. It irks you, creates this massive bubble of steaming water that wants to spill over. We all have been there, don't worry. It is that feeling when what they have said is so mean or just dumbfounded that we ball up our fists, sigh, smile, and nod our heads; that frustration that is about to explode; the emotion of complete and utter anger that fills us and consumes us. But we can deal with that emotion. It takes time to perfect it but staying calm, especially when the narcissist you are around is persistent in his or her presentation of themselves, can be a life-changing tool in being at peace with the situation or interaction. Sure, it is extremely difficult but acceptance of that situation or interaction with the narcissist and then finding a small piece of calm within you can certainly go a long way. For instance, a narcissist starts explaining all that you did wrong, whether this narcissist is someone at work or your loved one, and you become awash with anger but know how the narcissist will react, do you shout and go off and get nowhere with the narcissist or do you try your best to stay calm, listen, and then just move on? Everybody snaps eventually and that is our human nature, our survival instincts kicking in. It is a normal reaction. It is the pressure building up and our tempers becoming unhinged. But, we do need to be aware that by arguing with or retorting back at a narcissist only affects you and not them.

Try Not to Take the Narcissist's Actions Personally

To the narcissist, it's never actually about you. To him or her, you are a pawn in a mind game that they are playing, and if you weren't there, they would be doing the exact same thing to someone else. Of course, this doesn't make their abuse less painful, but at least, it clarifies things for you. It means that your suffering isn't a result of any wrongdoing on your part.

When your relationship or your association with a narcissist finally goes south you are going to start wondering how this person that you have known and trusted could have morphed into an entirely different and mean a person who you don't recognize at all. You will start thinking that maybe you did something to deserve their anger and their animosity. In your mind, you will feel that there has to be a rational explanation for what has happened. There is, of course, a psychological explanation for the things that are happening — but you can rest assured that you didn't play a part in making those things happen. They were just meant to happen, and they were never truly within your control.

The narcissist isn't hurting you or targeting you for a personal reason. You have nothing to do with it. The narcissist acts the way he/she does because that is the nature of the beast. It may seem callous, but it's true. The narcissist targeted you because you just happened to cross his/her path, or you just happened to be in their life.

This information doesn't make the suffering that you endured under the narcissist any less painful, but it has several important implications for you. First, it means that there is nothing wrong with you and that there is nothing that you did to deserve what the narcissist has done to you. Many people take the abuse of narcissists because they get accustomed to the suffering, and they start internalizing the idea that they might have done something to set off the abuse.

Don't delude yourself into thinking that the narcissist actually cares about you because what's happening is completely and utterly impersonal.

Chapter 7: Healing using Acceptance

You wonder if a relationship with the narcissist, no matter how painful it is for you, would be better than the hopelessness, because at least the face is the same. At the end of the grief stage comes acceptance. You have accepted that you cannot change the situation and that it is what it is. Even if you want nothing more than to change the situation, you know that reality is a reality, and you begin to move on. The pain may still be there, but you are slowly able to enjoy things again as you begin to heal.

Relationships can really shape your life regardless of if they are healthy or not. Every person in your life becomes a part of your experiences that you go through. Our experiences shape who we were, who we are today, and who is going to be or want to be. Every negative thing that you go through is an opportunity to implement positivity and engagement in self-growth. In healthy relationships, you are respected and honored without judgment.

When you get involved with a narcissist, quite the opposite happens. They make you become dependent on them, and take your strength from you, so that you feel trapped, or that you have to rely on you. This is their intention. Once this has taken place, and they have isolated you, and gotten you to a place of pure codependency, you feel as though you need them in your life. You feel as though even the abuse is hard, one day they will change if this, or if that. They won't then you are stuck in a vicious cycle living a nightmare. Acceptance is about accepting that the relationship is over, and you can gain this opportunity through no contact to do right for yourself.

Letting all hope go

The pattern that gets stuck on repeat from the narcissist is idolize, devalue, then discard. Without feeling any sense of empathy for you or your self-worth, the narcissist will cycle through this pattern indefinitely, leaving you feeling worthless. They put you on a pedestal and make you feel absolutely wonderful, then instantly drag you down, and discard your feelings by implementing blame. There is never a real conversation in between the arguments, and there are never real reasons they can give you to justify their behavior. This is never your fault. As long as you still hold what they need, or possess traits they can exploit, they will always hoover you or come back to poison you more.

The process of letting go of hope for them is that you can recognize this pattern, and reality should set in. If this sounds all too familiar, then all hope is lost for change, or "working things out." By holding onto this sense of hope, you are procrastinating your recovery, and sadly, it is false hope.

Addiction

With acceptance, you must understand that you are not "in love," or "holding on" for a reason. You are simply addicted to the emotions that the narcissist makes you feel. How much time do you spend a day thinking about the narcissist? How do you feel when they punish you for it? Think about the silent treatments, for example. Do you feel pain when you think about how they treat you as opposed to how you treat them? Do you feel insane? or even physically ill?

These feelings you feel have now caused you to feel addicted to them. It's called trauma bonding in which they implement to keep you around. To keep you thinking about them. In the idolizing phase, they keep you 'high' on the highs of the relationship through their actions, once they know everything is okay, and you are hooked all over again, they shift into the devaluation phase. Which is the mental abuse stage where they tell you everything that's wrong with you and can even set you up to do what they want you to do, so that when you do it, they can devalue you even more. Then, to keep you from running away, they implement little doses of love through the torture. Which sets you up to stay addicted. To recover, **no contact at all** is best.

By breaking this cycle through no contact, you can reprogram your own mind, and take control and power back from your abuser.

Heart, mind, and soul aid

Behaviors are driven by what you think, and how you feel or manage your emotions. Narcissistic abuse represents cognitive dissonance and denial. Cognitive dissonance means that you have conflicting beliefs to what you originally believed. Which results in confusion, distress, and to get out of it, you are driven to fix the contradiction you feel. So, this is why trust is necessary so that you don't question your beliefs, and you are confident that they cannot be countered by a narcissist. From the confusion of everything you once believed to now being everything you are unsure of if you should believe causes you to live in survival mode. In which you may feel depressed, anxious, panic, restless, lack of trust, paranoia, fear, social isolations, obsessive or intrusive thoughts, anger, night terrors, or nightmares, and numbness.

Whatever you feel, you cannot start your healing process until you work through the pain and every emotion that comes with the pain. This cannot happen until there are no more ties between you and the narcissist. From the moment you implement no contact with your narcissist, you can start to embrace the positive healing measure that you must take to become healthy again. Just remember, when you grieve and become devastated, you have started healing. It may not feel like it, but it's better this way.

Chapter 8: Building Self Esteem

If you had confidence before your relationship, then it is likely that the narcissist has taken that away from you. The most daunting task in your recovery process is to build a new sense of confidence, different than you had before. This can only come as you build your self-esteem and your perception of who you are and who you want to be. So, maybe you didn't have a bunch of confidence back then either, which is why it is crucial to start building it now so that you can feel what you do deserve - worthy and appreciated from yourself. The good news is that by following the last two suggestion, forgiving yourself, and learning to listen to your intuition, you will be also building self-awareness, which promotes confidence. Your goals through these three steps bring your awareness levels to a place where you can look at how the narcissist hurt you, and which areas you need to work on the most. Which will tell you your strengths and weaknesses, and in the process of working through your weaknesses, with every one you overcome, your confidence level will go up as well.

The process of building confidence cannot be completely done right unless you really look into the traumatic experiences you endured even before the narcissistic relationship. It could stem from childhood, and learn to break down, and walk through these barriers will help you see just how strong you really are, which will build a new level of confidence. Reaching out to support systems and teams like groups, classes, therapies, family, and friends, you will learn how to develop self-reflection. Self-reflection is crucial in learning more about yourself, and how you can see all the beautiful qualities the narcissist made you blind to. Take the pain that you feel, and use it to learn more about yourself, and you may just find out new things you never have seen about yourself before. By lighting up this whole new perception of yourself, you will find success and inner peace, which often leads to happiness.

Learning how to trust again is no easy task, but with patience and self-kindness, and the help of others, it is possible. When you have successfully learned how to reach inside yourself and trust who matters, then you can start putting your trust in new people who come into your life. This is because with the trust you feel inside yourself, you can trust that you know best when you are going to put your faith in someone else. This happens when you are perfectly in tune with your intuition. When you are in tune with your intuition, you will only follow your own gut instinct if you have the confidence to believe that you are right. And with forgiveness of your mistakes, you make along the way and patience to overcome whatever problems lie ahead for you, you will finally learn the true meaning of trust in yourself and in others.

When someone has low self-esteem, they are more vulnerable to narcissists and other people and situations that are largely negative. In fact, narcissists look for those with low self-esteem because they know that it will make it easier to get them into their web. When you have good self-esteem, you have a healthy level of self-respect and confidence in your abilities and worth. When self-esteem is low, someone is more likely to tolerate abusive situations, not live up to their potential and become depressed.

Self-esteem is a part of everything that you do in life. It affects your performance at school, work and in your relationships. Low self-esteem can also stop you from living a full life since it is characterized by fear to try new things or test your limits.

Self-esteem ultimately comes from within. However, there are a number of factors that can influence it. The people around you play a role in how you see yourself. This is especially true when it comes to those close to you and those you respect. For example, if a parent is constantly critical of a child, this can damage the child's self-esteem. On the other hand, when a parent is very supportive, it helps someone to see their own value which leads to healthy self-esteem.

Every person has that inner voice that essentially tells them what to think of themselves. For some, this inner voice can be highly negative and critical. When this happens, it is easy to believe the voice and feel as though you are inferior. It is common to have negative feelings, but when you allow them to dominate, you eventually start believing them. It is important to listen to negative inner feelings, but then put them into perspective. For example, you did poorly on a test, so naturally, this is upsetting. If your inner voice tells you that you are a failure and you listen to it and do not question it, you will start to believe this, resulting in lower self-esteem.

Comparing yourself to other people is another influencer on your self-esteem. It is fine to evaluate those around you, but do not allow this to overshadow your strengths. Taking inventory of your weaknesses and strengths and focusing on what you are good can help prevent the strengths of those around you from negatively impacting how you view yourself.

Improving Your Self-Esteem

The good news is that if you have low self-esteem, this does not have to remain. There are ways to boost it and alleviate the negative thoughts and feelings from dominating your view of yourself. To get started, work on developing life skills that contribute to how you see yourself and the world around you. These include:

- Do not be afraid to identify and experience your feelings. When you push feelings down and try to ignore them, they will eventually come to the surface.
- Do not be afraid to detach yourself from negative situations and people.

- Be receptive to those around you and empathize with people.
- Think optionally and not in black and white. This allows you to solve problems better and learn new things.
- Be assertive when it is needed. Do not allow others to dictate the direction of your life.

Focus on the good things in your life and what you are good at. Low self-esteem can make it seem like you are not good enough at anything. However, when you reflect on the good, it makes it easier to remember that it does exist on days when you are feeling down.

Make a learning opportunity out of every mistake. Every person fails and makes mistakes. This is part of life. However, do not dwell on these and the negative consequences that might come with them. Spend an hour being upset because it is important to experience your emotions. However, after an hour, go into action mode and consider why the mistake or failure occurred. You will always be able to find at least one lesson. This lesson reduces the risk of mistakes and failure in the future.

Know that perfection is simply not possible. What is important is that you are putting in the effort and working to learn and get better. No person is born automatically being great at everything. Life is all about learning and working on developing the skills needed to achieve your goals.

Remember that every person has their own strengths. Imagine a world where every person is just good at everything. There would be no healthy competition, no learning, and no balance. Know your strengths and respect the strengths of others.

Know what you cannot change. For example, if you are short, you are short. You cannot change this. Once you accept what cannot be changed, you can start putting your focus on the areas of your life that can be improved.

Do not be afraid to try. You never know what you are good at until you test your limits. Have you always wanted to play soccer, but were afraid you were not good enough? Get a game going with friends or join a local team. You may be great, or you may not. Either way, you tried it, and every new thing you try expands your horizons.

Give yourself credit when you deserve it. When you do something great, be proud of yourself. It is easy to put more focus on flaws because this is just what humans do. However, when you switch your focus to the good stuff, your self-esteem will get a boost.

Chapter 9: Common techniques to recovering yourself

No Contact

One of the first steps you can take is to cut off all ties, use the no contact rule - no matter what. Then it's all about self-care, and making a routine for yourself, like exercise which will greatly help you with the pain and stress you are feeling. Perhaps, the first and most important thing to do when getting through a narcissist break up is to cut off ties completely. This means absolutely no contact - no matter what. Look at it as a no-contact order, except you are giving yourself this. Having no contact may hurt at first, but if you keep with it, it can really teach you things like self-respect, self-discipline, and will give you the much-needed space and time to do you for a while. As you got through the waves on devastation, some days may be harder, so it may be best to come up with a safety phrase when you are having trouble fighting the urge to reach out. Phrases like "he will just continue to hurt me if I reach out" or "What's the benefits of talking to them? It will do me no good, and I will be back where I started." You are so fragile at this point in time, so having no contact will give you both time to accept that it's really over, so you both can move on.

No contact may seem really difficult, or almost impossible, simply because they are all you know, you have lived your life with them whether they were a spouse, parent, or friend, and now it feels strange to live without them. You may be half in and half out about doing what you need to do to get better because you still have beliefs things could work. The mantra you need to repeat to yourself is, "narcissists won't change, because they can't unless they are willing to accept they are a narcissist." Which they won't because they don't see that there even is a problem. However, if no contact is not an option, there are other things you can do to avoid them. If you are co-parenting with them, then safety precautions need to be taken, and if they are a family member where you will see them at family events, you need to set serious boundaries.

Talk Therapy

Trauma, especially from abuse from someone you loved and trusted, can be quite damaging to a person. You may feel as though you struggle to cope at times, or that some of your insecurities that the narcissist has installed are so deeply ingrained that you will never be able to get out from underneath them. Maybe you have no clear idea of where to go with your healing and you feel like you need guidance. No matter what, whether you are coping with your abuse better or worse than average, you could benefit from seeking therapy.

With a licensed professional by your side, you will be gently, and without judgment, guided through the healing process with someone that is prepared to talk you through what you are going through. You will have someone who can provide real, valuable feedback to you about why you think the way you do or what causes you to act in such a way by your side, holding your hand as you work through healing. This can be absolutely invaluable, especially if your partner was particularly abusive, or if you find yourself struggling with thoughts of self-harm, suicide, or feel as though your mental health may be suffering.

If you feel like getting involved with therapy would be a good option for you, you should start by asking your primary care physician for a referral in your area, or you can search for therapists in your area on the internet. Do not be deterred because you think therapy is stigmatized—there is nothing wrong with taking care of yourself, even if doing so involves getting a professional involved. Remember, no one would think twice if you went to a doctor if you broke your ankle and struggling with your mental health should be seen no differently. You can do this if you put your mind to it, and you should never let other people make you feel like you are making the wrong choice.

Acts of Kindness

Acts of kindness go hand in hand with self-awareness methods like how to be in the now with being mindful. Being mindful of your thoughts, feelings, and behavior can really help you to understand the behavior and feelings of others and has many more benefits.

Acts of kindness mean that you do things for other people, for no reason, and having no expectation of getting it in return. Kindness is contagious in the very aspect that people who witnessed the act of kindness become inspired or motivated to want to do the same thing. This will make the chances of 'paying it forward' increase at a higher level. Then when you do something kind for someone else, you will also feel good, as it causes a feel-good emotion to stem right in the base of your brain. When you do kind things for other people in front of a group of people, you have just caused a domino effect, because they will feel inspired to do the same thing.

Emotional Freedom Techniques-EFT

EFT stands for Emotional Freedom Techniques. EFT is used to help heal and recover from narcissistic abuse. This technique does not need to be guided by a professional therapist and can be done all on your own, wherever, and whenever you need.

EFT was founded by Gary Craig who was a Stanford trained engineer which he studied multiple acupressure techniques used for healing. The problem was that acupressure from what therapists used were complicated combinations of acupuncture points. So, Craig developed an easy formula called "tapping" on main acupressure/puncture points while concentrating on a problem. Using the system Craig found, happens to be considered effective for issues like anxiety, depression, abuse, phobias, and even PTSD or physical illnesses.

You will need numerous sessions of EFT to heal from narcissistic abuse. There are layers to EFT, which is called "aspects." EFT can heal some problems, as shown above, instantly, for in-depth or deeper issues. You will need to undergo the "aspects" of EFT to fully or almost fully heal from narcissistic abuse. After tapping on one aspect, or layer using EFT, if you don't find it helpful, try a different layer or aspect until you find the right fit.

Eye Movement Desensitization and Reprocessing-EMDR Therapy

It reduces the physiological distress accompanied by traumatic memories or flashbacks. This is when participants intentionally focus on their memories, while at the same time concentrating their attention outside themselves. It is a way to control your memories instead of them controlling you.

If done successfully, you teach your brain that you are no longer back there, and you are an adult now looking at your memories in a third person type of view. They ask you how you feel about the memory, and then ask you how you feel now. Then gradually get you to feel different about your memory and perceive it differently so you can get relief from the power or control it has over you now.

Narcissists implement all types of abuse to get what they want. It's basically the means of what most people think about when they hear the word abuse. However, narcissistic abuse is dangerous, and the recovery may not be healed in a few short sessions of EMDR because the damage that is done is worse than the damage that stems from normal abuse. Narcissists will add a layer of abuse on top of the "normal" abuse because they intentionally deceive you, brainwash you, repeat certain behaviors to trap you, and so forth. They mess with someone's core identity and make them believe something other than what they are supposed to or brought up believing.

You can never tell what a narcissist's true intentions are, whether they are telling the truth or not, who they really are, what their pasts were like, what they think about, basically everything you will question yourself about when it comes right down to who they are. When you ask questions, they may seem irritated, or allow you to know the minimum details. They lie not just to others and you, but mainly to themselves. The same methods or tactics used in cults, a narcissist will use to brainwash their partners or victims.

Positive Affirmations

Positive affirmations are phrases or statements that challenge negative or unhelpful thoughts. Basically, you come up with something motivating, inspiring, or something that builds your self-esteem and you repeat it. Kind of like a mantra. These affirmations can be encouraging, motivational, or anything positive that boosts your confidence and promotes a positive change in your life. If you want to make a long-term change about the way you feel and think, positive affirmations are what you need to practice daily.

When you talk nicely and be kind to yourself every day, you will start to love yourself for who you are, which creates a reversal effect of what the narcissist has made you believe. This creates a strong mental state in which you become more resilient to hurt, blame, and harmful inflictions inflicted on you from this point forward. Tell yourself the following affirmations daily, and you will regain a sense of empowerment, and speed up your recovery process.

Here are a few examples of affirmations for someone healing from narcissistic abuse:

- I deserve love and respect.

- I am happy with who I am right now and I accept myself, along with all of my flaws. Imperfection is perfectly normal and I accept that.

- Every day, every hour, I am one step closer to healing and one step further along my journey. It is always worth putting another step forward, even in the face of adversity.

- My perception of reality is accurate and believable, and I should trust it, no matter what.

- I am good enough the way I am today, but I should always strive to better myself for tomorrow.

- I am healing gradually. One day at a time. One step at a time.

- I am focusing on my future while leaving the past behind

- I am loved and will be loved. I deserve love, care, affection, and respect

- I am making myself a priority through self-care

- I know and trust myself

- I have created strict boundaries that I am going to stick to

- I have the support of the most important people in my life

Aromatherapy

Aromatherapy is a healing treatment that comes in the form of oil, called "essential oils." The oils are extracted from plants to promote health and well-being. It has gained more recognition for the science of medicine and healing. Aromatherapy has been used for healing purposes for thousands of years, stemming back to ancient cultures in China, India, and Egypt, among many other places. The natural plant extract can calm in balms, resins, and oils, and are known to have positive physical and psychological benefits.

Chapter 10: Common Tips and Tactics to Help You Get Your Life Back

Now that you have recognized all the ways that narcissistic abuse has impacted your relationship, it is time to start thinking about how you can get your life back. Fortunately, it is not as difficult as you think. Countless people have survived narcissistic abuse, and so can you. Here are some tips to help you do this.

Take steps to regain your confidence

One of the more powerful aspects of narcissistic abuse is that it breaks down your confidence. That is the goal: to tear you down in such a way that you become totally dependent on the narcissist. Therefore, one of the more important steps you can take is actually regaining your confidence. As you start to feel better about yourself, you will come to see the narcissist for who he or she is.

Keep your guard up

The narcissist uses the tools you give them against you. In other words, the narcissist knows how to manipulate you because you have taught them how to. They know all about you, even how your brain processes information. Although you cannot take back all the data that you have given this person, you can learn how to protect yourself in the future. Being a little reserved can go a long way.

Start spending more time around other people

The narcissist seeks to isolate you, so they can keep you in the codependent relationship. This is an aspect of narcissistic relationships that some people do not understand. As cruel as the narcissist can be, they actually need you around because you serve an important function for them. So what's the best way to disrupt their narcissistic pattern? Start spending more time around other people. This will give you a sense of your self-worth and help break the control the narcissist has over you.

Regard your needs as important, too

Your needs are just as important as those of your partner. You are not a robot who just needs a little bit of oil and some fuel, and that's it. You have physical and emotional needs, too, and your relationship should be meeting those needs. You are one of two people in a relationship, not the unfortunate person in chattel slavery or indentured servitude. Start regarding your own needs as important as those of your partner's and not secondary.

Take a Time-out

By giving yourself time to cool off, you keep yourself from exploding or making the situation exponentially worse by saying something you do not mean in your anger. The time out can have a specific time limit, such as asking for a week of space or can be indefinite with you waiting until you no longer feel like screaming every time you see the narcissist. The important thing here is to set the time limit to what you need rather than catering to anyone else or compromising on the length.

Cut off the narcissist

Similar to taking a time-out, cutting off the narcissist involves taking a step back from the situation altogether. However, unlike a time-out, cutting off is typically a permanent severance of the relationship. The only way to truly avoid any more harm, whether emotionally or physically, is to refuse to engage or associate with the narcissist completely. By never being near the narcissist or never acknowledging the narcissist, the narcissist never has the opportunity to hurt you.

Refusing to engage with the narcissist also comes with a secondary benefit: you have cut off the narcissist's strongest motivator. By refusing to be a source of the narcissistic supply he craves, the narcissist eventually loses interest in you and instead of moving onto someone else who will provide him with his fix.

Disengage Emotionally

By disengaging emotionally, you hear what he says and briefly acknowledge it, but do not take it seriously. Just as you would not care much when an angry child calls you a doo-doo head, you should not care much when the narcissist screams that you are a horribly selfish person that would be better off dead because at least then, more than one person would benefit from your life insurance or estate. While it can be hard to ignore what the narcissist says, especially if the narcissist is someone you have held in high regards in the past, such as a spouse or a parent, you must remember that it is not true. By refusing to become upset at the narcissist's accusations, you protect your self-esteem, and when you refuse to fall victim to the narcissist's tactics, the narcissist slowly loses interest in you as well.

Manage your expectations

Narcissists lack empathy. They certainly expect sympathy from others, but will seldom reciprocate. This absence of empathy makes it difficult for a narcissist to develop close and intimate bonds with others. You need to learn to accept and make peace with this. So, stop seeking empathy or compassion from the narcissist and instead try to manage your expectations.

Find Your Self

To find your self again, you need to step back and view yourself from afar. This means evaluating your current state in detail and then looking at that evaluation from an objective distance.

The best way to do this is to remove your thoughts and emotions from your own mind and put them somewhere else, where you can examine them more clearly. A great way to do this is to begin a daily journal, pouring all your emotions and the thoughts you've had onto paper. Make sure to concentrate on how you feel, not just on the events that made you feel that way.

Rebalance Your Life

A more formal version of this rediscovery of who you are and what you want is to reintroduce balance into your life. This is about what you need as well as what you want and involves rebuilding a balance that may have been toppled by your abuser's actions.

Your abuser may have removed your connection to friends, they may have insisted you live and work in places that weren't really your choice, they may have chosen your hobbies for you by demanding you do the things they wanted to do. One or more areas of your life may currently be lacking equilibrium, and it's time to bring that back.

The areas you will need to look at include:

- Your career (or future career if you are still in school)
- Your relationships
- Your living situation
- Your hobbies and interests
- Your beliefs

First, you will need to look at each of these areas in turn and ask yourself how the abuse affected them. Once you have determined what changed in these areas of your life thanks to the abuse, you can think about what you want instead – and then make those changes happen. As you do, think about the boundaries you want to set. Tell yourself what you will and won't accept from outside influence in the future.

Calm your mind

Find a quiet place, close the door, turn the phone off or put it on silent, and physically distance yourself from all devices. Then take a few deep and relaxing breaths. Concentrate on inhaling and exhaling. Whenever thoughts float in your head, imagine them as clouds floating in the sky. Then you can redirect your attention and concentrate on your breathing. Call it meditation if you like, but it's an excellent technique to calm the mind. When your mind is calm, you can think better and listen to your intuition again. Not just that, it also helps you think more rationally.

Listen to your intuition

Pay attention to what your instincts tell you, especially when you meet someone for the first time. Your body is good at understanding the vibes you get from others. It might not be a full-fledged science, but it does help you get a read on things and the people around you. Pay attention to what you feel as soon as you meet someone; focus on the instant reaction you feel before you have even had the time to think. This will help you to understand whether you are comfortable with someone or not.

Pay attention to your body signals

Your body tends to provide you with messages about your health, the decisions you make, and others around you. Learn to start paying attention to these signals that your body keeps giving. But, it means that you must rest when tired, cry when you are sad, eat when you are hungry, and take a break when you are stressed out. It also means that you should start taking note of those around you who help to boost your energy levels and those who extinguish them. You can use this information while deciding whether someone is a good influence on you or not. This will help you limit your contact with people who feel toxic.

Take a step back and analyze the situation.

Determine how bad the situation is. Try to understand the narcissist's background and his degree of his narcissism. Note or recall what drives him to narcissistic rage. Recall how he tries to punish you. Be aware of the tactics that he uses. Do all these objectively. Being carried away by emotions, shouting or crying will only feed the narcissist. The narcissist has already painstakingly set up a strong image or reputation and you might not come across as credible when you tell others, so you have to do your homework.

Accept that the narcissist will not change.

Hoping that you will be able to knock some sense into the narcissist or that you could explain and things to enlighten him will not work. As far as the narcissist is concerned, he has done no wrong.

Seek help.

Find people – friends, counselors, religious leaders, or parents- any one you can confide in and who can give advice and emotional support. They can also give feedback from a neutral viewpoint.

Relaxation

Relaxation is an important part of everyone's lives, including the narcissist. But for us who are dating or married to a narcissist, friends with one, or the narcissist happens to be your mother or father, finding time to get away from the hounding madness that usually ensues when in their company is a valuable asset in managing your emotional and mental strength. Constantly listening can switch you off, make you feel unmotivated, and hurt you. It can drive you mad and can drive you away in tears. But finding somewhere where you can essentially switch off and switch back on again is paramount. Hiking, running, a beach walks. Clarity is the best natural and mental healer. It allows for storage space to be freed up and offers you the platform to think. Reading a book, listening to music, cooking. There are so many forms of relaxation that can really refresh someone. Renew yourself away from the narcissistic atmosphere and remove yourself from the narcissistic environment in which you live or work in. Even if this is for ten minutes, finding that balance again is important when dealing with a narcissist.

Be realistic.

Know the narcissist's limitations and work within those limits. It will only be emotionally draining and a waste of time to expect more from the narcissist than he is capable. Do not expect him to learn to care because he can't. Remember that your value as a person does not depend on the narcissist. Don't punish yourself for getting into a relationship with him. Instead, focus on rebuilding your self-esteem, meeting your own needs and pursuing your interests.

Set Your Boundaries and Stick to Them

You need to set boundaries. If you want the process of healing to begin, you must establish a protective wall around yourself. If you can put physical distance between yourself and the narcissist, that's great! Memories related to the narcissist and the relationship will certainly trigger pain and other unpleasant emotions that in turn will slow down your progress. So, cut off all ties with the narcissist. You can block that individual on social media, your phone, and even an email list. It is time to get rid of all the things that remind you of the narcissist. It is time to remove all traces of connection with the narcissist.

Make Sure to Stay Positive

Narcissists feed on watching other people feel bad, so even if they do cause you to experience negative emotions, do not let them see this. When you are around them, make sure that you are in a positive mindset. No matter how hard they try to bring you down, keep a smile on your face and do not react to them.

Know That They Need Help

Narcissism is a mental health issue that someone cannot just will away. They will need help if they ever expect to get their behavior under control. If you approach them and recommend they reach out to a professional, they are unlikely to just agree and go. They may even become angry or defensive due to you even suggesting it. If you care about the person and want them to at least consider help, approach the subject gently and know that this is something that you will likely have to discuss several times before they will even consider it.

Freeing Yourself from Negative Emotions

Anger, jealousy, envy and other negative emotions can permeate your life and cause significant problems. It is important to recognize their existence and then work to be free of them. Freeing yourself from such emotions is a process, and it takes time. Even after you free yourself, you will need to commit to long-term work and maintenance.

Negative emotions are powerful and can quickly become habits if you do not get them under control. For example, if you commonly respond to criticism with anger, over time, this repetition will cause you to become angry any time you are criticized. This can start to impact your relationships, your career and other elements of your life.

Stop Making Excuses

When you make excuses for negative emotions, either for yourself or others, you are telling yourself that they are something out of your control. This is not true because you have the choice concerning how you react to a situation. If you continue to make excuses, you will never take responsibility for your behavior. Over time, this can start to push people out of your life because they will not want to be around someone who cannot admit their faults or when they are wrong.

Take Responsibility

Once you dedicate yourself to no longer making excuses, you can start to take some responsibility for how you act in various situations. This starts by taking the power away from your negative emotions. As you continue to take responsibility, you will find that they lose their hold over you. The right reactions and choices will naturally start to become easier to make.

Let It Go

Life would be much simpler if everything could be controlled, but this is not possible. When you find something that you have no control over, recognize it and let it go. For example, not every person will like you, and there are times when a loved one may get mad at you for something that is not your fault. Do not press the issue. Let it go, and everything will eventually work itself out in the end.

There are simpler things that you can start doing on a regular basis to start pushing out negative emotions and helping to enhance your overall well-being. You do not have to do every single one on a daily basis but consider them and incorporate them into your day when it is appropriate.

Get your Life Back on Track

It can be tricky to stop dwelling in the past and to stop thinking about all the pain the narcissistic abuse caused. You need to stop pondering about the past and instead focus on the bright future ahead. Experiencing pain is the natural response to abuse, and it might have also damaged your sense of self. So, you are dealing with a lot. Getting your life back on track after a narcissistic injury or after ending a relationship with a narcissist is not an easy task. There exists a cognitive discord between two ideas that causes a lot of confusion when the relationship ends. One part of your brain might still be thinking about the narcissist as your soul mate while the other party views him as your ex. This discord causes confusion, and often those who were victims of narcissistic abuse or were in a toxic relationship with a narcissist are usually in disbelief. It's a disbelief that someone they trusted violated his trust and abused his love.

Be patient

You must be patient with yourself. You cannot hurry up and rush through the process of recovery. There will be times when you feel like you are staring at a bottomless pit of despair; you might get frustrated or might even feel quite depressed. Well, this merely means you need to concentrate on healing yourself.

Conclusion

If you have made it to the end of the book, that's a huge first step toward recognizing the abuse that a narcissist in your life may be inflicting. You have taken the time and effort to begin questioning your relationship, and that is the first step in this journey. That is the beginning toward acknowledging the abuse that you have endured, and such a monumental step should be acknowledged and celebrated.

Narcissistic abuse is perhaps one of the most extreme and damaging relationships you could ever experience due to the power they hold over you, and then the work you need to do to get better afterward. So, take your trauma, and look at it as an opportunity to do something better for yourself. Be that strong, confident person you have always wanted to be. Do the work it takes to get the fulfillment you need. Fight the fear of change and ask yourself the important questions that will move you forward. Do I want to live in a bad relationship forever? What is the main benefit to me by allowing this behavior to happen? Who do I want to be? Everything you possibly imagined that you could have wanted is why you are in a narcissistic relationship. It is why you grabbed this book and read it to the end. Where you are in your life right now is exactly where you are supposed to be. The next step is what you choose. What kind of change will you make for yourself right now? What decisions will you make to make your future brighter?

Don't underestimate the power of the human mind to overcome even the most hurtful of emotional experiences. There are many different ways survivors can choose from on their paths to recovery. The key is to believe in yourself and trust in your instincts and gut feelings fueling you forward and past any and all symptoms of narcissistic abuse.

Remember to always keep your eye out for red flags and acknowledge them in the moment and trust your gut instinct when you feel like something might be alarming. You should always trust your instinct, as it is often your first warning that something is not quite right.

You are a survivor of your situation and with the tools within this book arming you, you will be able to protect yourself. Remember, if you feel physically unsafe in your relationship, it is always acceptable to call for help. There are domestic violence hotlines that can help you locate resources and help you get out if you feel like that is your best option in that moment. You should ultimately seek to do what is best for you, making sure you are taken care of. Do not hesitate to call out for help, and do not feel ashamed for the actions of the narcissist. They do not reflect poorly on you.

As you navigate through this tough time, remember that you are strong. Ending your relationship makes you strong. Seeking help and support to survive makes you strong. You are a fighter, willing to push back and refuse to accept the abuse the narcissist attempted to use against you. You are not broken, unworthy, valueless, or weak. You are strong. You are a survivor. You deserve the happiness and peace of mind.

Good luck in your Healing journey.

Emotionally Immature Parents

A Healing Guide to Overcome Childhood Emotional Neglect due to Absent and Self Involved Parents

Karen Hart

EMOTIONS

The science in search of the feeling

What are emotions? A clear and universal definition does not exist so far. To date, science relies only on working definitions - more comparable to a description of a phenomenon than to a definition in the true sense.

If for some, they are pure stimulus-response patterns triggered by environmental conditions, others see it as a neurophysiological reaction that occurs only in the brain and that we can not control.

Still, others argue that emotions are a social construction. Ultimately, the social environment that characterizes us depends on the feelings we have in certain situations.

To get the emotions on the track, generations of scientists took a look into the brain. What happens in this organ that makes us feel? However, this can not be seen in the normal view of a brain. Tissue sections also give the researchers insights into the structure of this organ, but they offer little insight into how it works.

In the mid-twentieth century, experiments involving plants such as a rooster and an electrode were planted in the brain as a ground-breaking experiment. Electrical stimuli were used to stimulate different areas of the brain, causing reactions such as aggression and combat readiness, anxiety, hunger or thirst.

But the question of what emotions are now could not really answer these investigations. Especially since in this time, the general opinion was held that animals possess at most innate instincts. Real emotions, on the other hand, were reserved for humans only. An opinion that has changed fundamentally.

Feeling sets the path

So what's up with feeling? Biologically, emotions are complex behaviours that have evolved over the course of evolution. But why do we need them?

Emotions help us to orient ourselves in everyday life. We make many decisions "on the stomach". We are constantly experiencing this, even if we are not aware of it.

Even if we want to weigh rationally and let reason decide, it is often this first impulse that leads us to one or the other decision.

Our emotions are a rating system that can be more or less well-endowed. It is not complete from the start but is constantly being expanded and refined through our everyday experiences. Nothing we experience has no effect.

Thus, for someone who has never suffered a loss, the term grief will not matter much. On the other hand, the more significant the loss that hits a person, the greater will be the feeling of grief and pain.

Every experience we make, everything we learn, is linked in the brain to the feeling we feel in this situation.

The more intense this feeling is, the more it remains anchored in our memory. The experience becomes part of our life experience. The greater this wealth of experience, the more different our emotional rating system becomes.

Emotion and physical reaction are inseparable

Every feeling is always accompanied by a physical reaction. We can smile or laugh. We can even laugh so much that tears come to our eyes. We cry for joy, out of emotion, or because we are sad.

And, of course, we can also see from these physical reactions how other people are doing. We can only understand them by their body language - without words.

This interaction between our thoughts, emotions and our body is inextricably linked. Scientists speak of the somatic markers. They can also be measured in laboratory tests. The subjects are shown different pictures — sensors on the face record muscle reactions.

Each time the subjects see emotionally charged images, a particular muscle above the eyebrow responds. The same thing happens when unpleasant thoughts are called. In neutral images or positive thoughts, on the other hand, this muscle game is out.

We are constantly experiencing this embodiment of feelings. Often, however, they only really become aware of us when they are strong. For example, if we are so scared that our hair is upside down when we have a lot of excitement or have to go to the next toilet. The love announces itself with palpitations and "butterflies in the belly".

It is also possible to reverse this effect of somatic markers. In the same way as feelings influence our body, we can also influence our feelings with conscious postures. For example, anxiety or stress often causes us to huddle together, cramping our bodies.

When we become aware of it, we can sit up, take a deep breath and feel better. Investigations have even shown that pessimistic people who are traveling with a grumpy face, have a less well-perfused back.

THE PARENTAL IMMATURE

The first typology refers to those parents and those mothers with erratic and uneven behaviour. They are emotionally unstable parents, of those who make promises that do not keep today and tomorrow. Parents who are very present today and tomorrow let their children feel that they are annoying.

Impulsive parents, on the other hand, are those who act without thinking, who make plans without considering the consequences, ranging from error in error and recklessness in recklessness without weighing their actions.

Motherhood and passive fatherhood is undoubtedly one of the clearest examples of immatureness. They are the ones who do not get involved, those who are present but who are absent and those who base their upbringing.

Finally, it is also common for the figure of derogatory parents, those who make their children feel that they are annoying or unwanted, those who understand parenting as something that surpasses them and that they do not want to be part of.

These four profiles sculpt with disappointment, a youth truncated, injured and declared invalid. Every child that grows up in this context will experience clear feelings of abandonment, loneliness, frustration and anger.

The risk of being a mother or father present, but absent The father or mother present, but absent, is not emotionally accessible, and all this has serious consequences for the child. Read more "

Children who become adults: wounds that heal

We pointed to the beginning: the child who grew up under the assumption that it is an adult role does not always take on a stronger, more mature or even less happy role. Leaving on the shoulders of a small child of 8, 10 or even 15 years of age the exclusive responsibility to take care of themselves, a younger brother, or decisions that their parents should make, leaves a stamp and maybe the cause of many shortcomings.

The psychological consequences that usually prevail in these cases are as varied as complex: emotional loneliness, self-confidence, inability to enter into solid relationships, feelings of guilt, emotional limitation, suppression of anger, fear, irrational thoughts ...

Overcoming these injuries due to a lost childhood and immature parents is not an easy task, but it is not impossible. Cognitive behavioural therapy is very useful, as is the acceptance of the existence of that wound caused by neglect or neglect. Later, the needy reconciliation will come to us, allowing us to feel anger and frustration for a stolen youth and forcing us to grow too fast or leave us too early.

We have lost childhood, but Life opens up for us, delicious, free and always tasty to enable us to be what we have always wanted and that we undoubtedly deserve. Let us make sure that our parents' emotional immunity does not prevent us from developing the present and future happiness that we have not received in the past.

To be or not to be

To be or not to be, this is the question. Being a parent is a responsibility. A big responsibility We live in a society in which we are dragged by social inertia. Studying, working, having a partner, getting married, having children, continuing to work ... Many couples have children because that is what is expected. Because society requires that you have children at a certain age.

Other couples don't expect to have it in extremis, but they want it because they are convinced that it is the next step in their lives and they have it.

Having children is an important decision. So you don't have to take it motivated by the rush, or by " must-have ". But if you have a child to raise, give love, attention, love, upbringing ...

CHILD OF A NARCISSIST

It falls under the primal needs of a child to be loved, respected and taken seriously from the very beginning in everything it is: in what it looks like, how it feels and how it expresses itself. Only when a child feels safe to be himself, can he gradually separate from his parents in a healthy way and grows into an emotionally mature person.

Emotionally immature parents

But if a parent himself has not had parents who could give him this love, warmth and respect, he is often 'needy' himself. That is, looking for something he could not get from his parents: someone who gives him love and security understands it and takes it seriously.

Unmet need

If such a need remains unconscious, and the parent does nothing to develop and heal himself, he will (unconsciously) continue to try to satisfy his unmet need in all sorts of surrogate ways. He or she seeks that satisfaction by seeking confirmation from persons who, as it were, represent the parents, such as the partner and the children.

The child takes care of his needy parents

The own children, in particular, are 'suitable' for this. After all, a child is available and 'malleable': you can raise it so that it becomes the way you want it. And because a child is completely at the mercy of his parents and his life literally depends on their attention and love, it is more than willing to adapt to the needs of his parents. A child feels exactly what his parents need and, in exchange for their 'love' and approval, gives them intuitively and unconsciously the respect, attention and admiration they ask for.

If a parent has felt weak and powerless as a child, he can now feel strong by asserting his power; he can require the child to listen to him and show respect for him. The parent can finally feel that he is the centre of attention.

Suppress own needs and feelings

A child of 'needy' parents learns to adapt at a very young age and thus to suppress their own need for love, respect and compassion, as well as unwanted emotions such as fear, abandonment, anger, powerlessness and jealousy. It starts to think negative thoughts about itself as "It is up to me that Mama does this." Children naturally place the blame on themselves.

Defence mechanisms

These are known defence mechanisms with which a child protects himself against painful experiences. By repressing or distorting the truth, creating an illusion, the child bridges the gap between his deep desire for loving parents who see him for who he is and the reality, namely a father or mother projecting their own needs onto the child. Only in this way can the child survive, but it also builds a wall around itself. By denying the unwanted parts of itself, it loses (a part of) itself.

False itself

All this can (but does not have to!) Lead to the development of a so-called unreal self: the child and later the adult show purely and only what is expected of him by his parents. You can imagine that these children of needy parents themselves become needy parents who constantly need confirmation from their environment.

Causes of narcissism

Although there is disagreement about the causes of narcissism and, for example, there are people who claim that there is a genetic component, narcissism is essentially about the loss of the true self and the creation of an unreal self.

And that can, of course, have the various causes that people point to as causes of narcissism. For example, it is said that neglect, abuse or trauma can cause. But also, for example, children who are idealized by their environment and are not held responsible for their actions. In all cases, the child feels compelled to deny and protect himself.

Normal families

In addition, they speak of studies in which narcissists came from normal families. But what is a 'normal' family anyway? After all, there are enough families in which lack of respect for the individuality of the child, (subtle) manipulation and performance pressure are considered 'normal'. And these children, once they have grown up, say more than once that they have had a great childhood with parents who wanted them the best, by no means always realizing that they had to deny (part of) themselves for that.

Deeply hurt child

If you realize that behind the person suffering from a narcissistic personality disorder, there is actually a deeply hurt child who has had to deny himself and create an unreal self to survive, then you better understand that you cannot actually talk about good guy (the victim) and a bad guy (the narcissist). The narcissist himself was once a victim, although you cannot, of course, justify narcissistic behaviour in any way and it remains important that you distance yourself from it.

The narcissism label

Although I use the label 'narcissist' and 'narcissism' myself because it can give a lot of clarification and people simply search the internet for this term, I therefore also have my objections to its use. The 'narcissist' label does not do justice to the injured and scorned child hiding behind the facade. Contempt is heard, while contempt (namely the contempt for the child it once was) has caused the child to have to deny himself.

A label also has no gradations and gives no room for the possibility to grow or change: you are a narcissist, or you are not. But that is not entirely the case. Everyone has narcissistic traits, and everyone has had to deny parts of themselves. As already stated elsewhere, narcissism is a spectrum disorder: there are gradations in how far someone has moved away from themselves. And if the wall that someone has built around them is very thick, it is because there is a very thick layer of pain and sorrow underneath. Not everyone dares to take on that pain. That explains why narcissists are often not open to therapy or continue their narcissistic games during therapy.

Although I will continue to use the terms 'narcissist' and 'narcissism' because otherwise, it will be difficult to write about it, it is, therefore, quite a complicated story that may be nuanced from time to time.

Child of a narcissist

As said before: by no means does every child of a narcissistic parent develop a narcissistic personality disorder (an unreal self), even though that possibility exists. However, a narcissist's child inevitably had to deny parts of himself, repressed emotions it had stored in the body, and acquired limiting beliefs early on.

Children of narcissists often suffer from feelings of inferiority that are difficult for them to find.

Release from your parents

These children usually find it hard to get rid of their parent: even at a later age they continue to adapt to their parent's wishes, or they apparently go their own way but can be deeply touched by the behaviour of their father or mother until a late age. They don't really feel free. Deep inside, they often hope to get the love and approval of their parents (or their partner or children!) That they have always longed for.

PERSONALITY DISORDER IN PARENT

Narcissism is one of the ten personality disorders that know clinical psychology and psychiatry. Although everyone has narcissistic traits, you only speak of a disorder if these traits take on an extreme form.

Egocentrism, vanity and self-righteousness

Egocentrism, vanity and self-righteousness are the keywords of this disorder. The world revolves around the narcissist, who, with his poor empathy, does not take others into account, thinks he can make anything and does not tolerate contradiction. He will never put his hand in his bosom: the fault is always with the other. Those who suffer narcissism feel superior, exaggerate their qualities and achievements. A narcissist is always looking for attention and confirmation and manipulates others to achieve his goal.

Narcissus

The word narcissism refers to a figure from Greek mythology, called Narcissus. He fell so in love with himself that he could no longer separate himself from the spot near the stream where he could admire his reflection in the water. He languished from unfulfilled longing for himself. The flower that bears his name sprung from where he had been.

Ideal image

The myth of Narcissus nicely portrays what the essence of narcissism is about. Narcissists are 'in love' with a perfect image that they have created of themselves. That ideal image can look in all sorts of ways, depending on the role they have chosen: it can be a successful businessman, but also an enlightened guru, or even a caring mother. That makes it so treacherous and not always easy to recognize, certainly also because a narcissist does not always (immediately) show his real face. They are often good actors who can seem very charming and social. With their lovely appearance, they try to pack everyone.

Lack of self-esteem

Behind the facade that the narcissist shows to the world, however, there is no happy and fulfilled person, even though he seems full of himself. He has a very poor sense of self-worth. But he has built such a thick armour around it that he is (often) no longer aware of his low sense of self. A narcissist really believes that he is what he wants to show the world, and he clings to this ideal image .

Confirmation

It is therefore not for nothing that he wants to see this image constantly confirmed by his environment. He demands a lot of attention: sometimes by fishing for compliments or by complaining and nagging. By only talking about himself and his interests or by being extremely dependent. Anyone who criticizes him or confronts him with reality gets the wind out. Because he feels unfulfilled and dissatisfied by definition, he cannot get enough attention and admiration. One of the characteristics that you can easily recognize a narcissist is its ability to extract all energy from you.

Different types of narcissism: open and hidden narcissism

A distinction is made between different subtypes in narcissistic personality disorder that not everyone agrees with. The distinction that is made most often is that between open and hidden narcissism. Where an open narcissist puts himself in the spotlight much more and does not hide his arrogance, a hidden narcissist keeps his delusions of grandeur more for himself, as a result of which he is only 'exposed' by his loved ones. The latter can present itself to the outside world as very friendly and thoughtful. Whatever type of narcissism it is, for them in the immediate vicinity of the narcissist, it is clearly felt that the world revolves around the narcissist.

Narcissists:

Are self-centred.

Feel better than another.

Require a lot of attention.

Enforce admiration.

Are never satisfied.

Eat energy.

Don't know guilt.

Project their own defects on others.

Manipulate and use others to achieve their own goals.

Are jealous and suspicious.

Want to exercise power over others.

Drive their way.

Prefer to talk about themselves or what interests them.

Do not listen to others.

Try to belittle another person or put him in a bad light.

Criticize others.

People play against each other.

Are extremely sensitive to criticism.

Think they can make anything.

Are out of contact with their deeper self.

Are negative and have little pleasure or sense of humour.

Have few adult qualities (rather the consciousness of a child).

Are focused on their own agenda.

Can lie crystal clear if it suits them.

Exaggerate their achievements and talents.

Need the energy of others to 'feed' with.

Thinking to have more rights than others.

Spectrum disorder

Of course, not every narcissist will show all these characteristics, nor can someone who has one or more of these characteristics be labelled as narcissists. It is important to handle this with care. Only a psychologist or psychiatrist can make such a diagnosis. Moreover, narcissism is a spectrum disorder. In other words, you have gradations in it. While it is still possible to live with one narcissist, he who is at the other end of the narcissism spectrum can be downright dangerous.

The mask of the narcissist

Why and how does a narcissist use the mask?

The mask offers the narcissist the opportunity to feel good about himself. He tells himself that he is someone else than he really is because it is painful for him to be confronted with his inner emptiness.

The mask serves to protect him from the moral judgment of ordinary people who are naturally not waiting for self-centred and unscrupulous behaviour. He does that by imitating them and displaying socially accepted behaviour if the situation demands it.

By posing differently or better than he is, the mask serves to attract attention to himself, to manipulate it and to seduce the other person in order to bind himself to him in a parasitic relationship. In the end, he needs the energy of the other to compensate for his own inner emptiness. He gets that energy through attention and admiration, but also by 'sucking someone empty' by bleeding him psychologically.

What does the mask look like?

The mask can look in all kinds of ways: from very ordinary, superior, sympathetic and charismatic, reasonable and conscientious, caring, to needy, hurt and pitiful. A narcissist does not always wear the same mask. Because the mask is empty and has no depth, it can easily be exchanged for another mask, depending on the circumstances.

Transparent or refined

The mask can be rather awkward and transparent, but it is often also particularly sophisticated and convincing. Because the mask is a matter of survival, the narcissist often puts a lot of energy into perfecting it. It is sometimes so good, including facial expressions, voice use, emotions and human flaws, that it is indistinguishable from real, not even by a professional.

Unsustainable

Because all this falsehood takes a lot of energy, a narcissist cannot keep it up all the time. There are times or periods when he lets go and shows his true nature. Or there is an environment where the narcissist wears the mask and another where the mask often goes off. Think of the charming, always friendly and available colleague who terrorizes her family at home. Or the perfect partner and father who misuses his position as a doctor, judge or teacher to cause suffering to people. The energy that he extracts from these people enables him to put on his 'good' mask temporarily.

The gap between reality and lie

The gap between reality and the lie (the mask) is sometimes so great that if someone finds out the true nature of the narcissist, he simply cannot believe it and continues to deny reality. The narcissist will also do everything to make the other person doubt himself if he confronts him with his discovery. It can sometimes take years for someone to see the slick façade of the narcissist fully. And then it can be quite a job to get rid of him.

Unmask a narcissist

Most people, however, look no further than the mask, simply because their contact with the narcissist is less intensive. If someone then shares his insights about the narcissist with his environment, this first one can sometimes be declared crazy:

"How can you speak angrily about such a nice person?" It often happens that conflicts arise between those who see through the narcissist and those who stand up for him. In the meantime, the person who caused it all, namely the narcissist himself, is watching hands from a distance.

Inverted world

Imagine the following situation:

A nice, respected woman has here and there informed her environment that her husband has psychological problems and that she is very concerned about him. Then this husband wants to divorce her, and he insists that he get custody of the children. The woman is visibly affected and says she is devastated. Nasty lawsuits follow, and the woman knows how to convince everyone of the lability of the man. Mutual friends choose the side of the woman. They think it is terrible that the man claims bad things about her, as the woman says, to get custody. After all, she is always so kind and cordial. The judge assigns the children to the woman. The man remains destitute.

Do you know who you would believe? Or would you say: where two fights have two guilt?

Victim and offender

It often happens that the narcissist appoints his victim (or the person he has aimed his arrows at) as perpetrator and steps into the role of the victim himself. He gratefully uses his mask to influence his environment and distort reality so that everything seems different than it is. In doing so, he often works extremely boiled and sly, by, for example, sowing doubts about the credibility of the victim, as in the situation above.

Double agenda

It will now be clear to you that narcissism cannot be recognized by a few superficial behavioural characteristics, but that the problem takes place at a much deeper level. Everyone can sometimes behave selfishly, and everyone can present themselves better than they are. The difference between a narcissist and a non-narcissist is the dual agenda of the first. A narcissist uses his mask (s) for the express purpose of taking and leaving the other destitute.

UNSAFE YOUTH

An unsafe childhood is sometimes unmistakable. For example, when children are abused and abused. And the numbers don't lie. No less than 80,000 children are abused in the Netherlands every year. So this is a fate that affects many children. But even children who are not exposed to very drastic and nasty experiences sometimes do not get what they need from their parents on a structural basis. Things you need to grow up to be a balanced adult.

Emotionally and pedagogically neglected

For the outside world, the more subtle form of an unsafe childhood is not always clearly visible. These are children who, for example, are emotionally and pedagogically neglected, verbally belittled or ignored. They witness a bad marriage, suffer from tensions from their parents or are used as a mainstay. The parents are not there for the children. In fact, the children must be there for the parents. And so do not get enough of their own development. We also call that an unsafe childhood.

The role of the parents

All parents know: good parenting is an art. It requires wisdom, endless patience and a lot of love. Moreover, love must express itself in loving behaviour, otherwise, it is an empty word. But nobody is perfect. So the art is to be good enough! To be mature enough and mentally healthy. Because when adult and psychologically healthy parents make mistakes in relation to their children, they admit the mistakes. They try to repair the damage and prevent a recurrence. The trust in the parent usually remains. Immature parents, on the other hand, do not see their own mistakes and deficiencies sufficiently and will ignore the children's complaints. The basic confidence of the child in the parents is then fundamentally and seriously damaged.

Unmet need

How does unsafe youth arise? Parents often bring children into the world from an unmet need. Consciously or unconsciously, they hope that the child will provide for their needs. Such as unconditional love. A child will want to meet those expectations because it loves its parents. No matter how unrealistic those expectations may be. Instead of living their own lives, they try to survive.

Consequences of unsafe youth

Does a child grow up in oppressive, neglecting circumstances? And did it have to build its life on defence mechanisms and survival strategies? Then that has consequences for the development of the personality. Vigilance, fear and sorrow, swallowed and forbidden anger often dominate. These children often develop depression and other disorders in adulthood. And start to behave in intimate relationships in an avoiding, repelling or disorganized way. This can lead to serious (relationship) problems. Life is difficult for them.

It must get out!

If you grew up in an unsafe family as a child, then your incriminating history is always present as an undercurrent in your adult life. It is a story, but a story without words. Children who have grown up unsafe have no texts to express themselves because they do not know the words. Only when they start to make a story out of it does the processing start. The wordless story must be told. It must get out! Often with the help of a (psycho) therapist. Telling the story is the first important step in the search for recognition and processing of history.

CHILDREN OF EMOTIONALLY IMMATURE PARENTS LOST THEIR CHILDHOOD.

Being the son of emotionally immature parents leaves deep marks. They are so many children who take on adult responsibility assume and that they are prematurely forced by this parental incompetence, by that vulnerable, neglected and negligent link that fades childhood and destroys self-esteem.

No one can choose their parents, we know, and although there is always a time when we, as adults, have the full right to choose the type of treatment we want to establish with them, a child cannot do it. Because being born is almost like falling from a chimney. There are people who are lucky enough to be reached by beautiful, competent and competent parents who will enable them to grow in a safe, mature and dignified manner.

On the other hand, there are people who have the misfortune to land in the arms of immature parents who will unyieldingly determine the foundations of their personality. Well, experts in child psychology and family dynamics know that in these cases, two very striking things can happen, as well as determine.

Parents with a clearly immature and incompetent personality can sometimes prefer to raise tyrannical and equally immature children. However, they can also encourage children to take on the role of that adult who has deterred parents from training. This is how some children ultimately take responsibility for their younger brothers and sisters, take care of household chores, or make decisions that are not of their age.

This last fact, however curious it may seem, will not make that child more courageous, more mature or more responsible in a way that we could understand as healthy. What is achieved above all is because of the beings of the world who have lost their childhood to give?

Emotionally immature parents, shortened childhood

Something we all agree on is that having children does not make us real parents. Motherhood, as the most healthy and meaningful paternity, is demonstrated by being present, offering a real, enriching and strong affection for that child to be part of Life and not a broken heart and only linked to fear, shortcomings and the low self-esteem.

Something that every child needs, in addition to simple food and clothing, is that emotional accessibility, Adult and Safe, where you feel connected to some people to understand the world and in turn understand yourself. If this fails, everything will fall apart. The child's own emotions are declared invalid by the emotionally immature father or by that mother who, only concerned about himself, neglects the feelings and emotional needs of the children.

On the other hand, it must be said that this type of dynamic is more complex than they seem at first sight so much that it is useful to distinguish 4 types of emotionally immature parents and mothers.

CHILDREN WITH EMOTIONALLY IMMATURE PARENTS

Children with emotionally immature parents are deeply scarred. Many of them ultimately assume the responsibilities of the adults, making them grow up way too fast. The combination of parental incompetence and neglect of that vulnerable bond causes the line between childhood and adulthood to become blurred for the children, which has a negative impact on their self-confidence.

We know that nobody can choose their parents. As adults, we have the right to decide for ourselves what kind of relationship we want to have with our parents, but a child does not yet have this right. Being born is just like falling out of the sky. Some are taken care of by wonderful and competent parents who educate us in a safe, mature and dignified manner.

Some, on the other hand, have enormous bad luck and end up in the arms of immature parents. And whether we like it or not, our parents determine the basis of our personality. Experts in the field of child psychology and family dynamics know that in these cases, two decisive and remarkable things can happen.

Parents who clearly have an immature and incompetent personality sometimes raise children who can be just as immature or tyrannical. Another possibility is that the children take on the role of the adults, who the parents refuse to fulfil.

As a result, it may happen that some children take care of their younger brothers and sisters, take care of the household or make choices that do not match their age at all.

This last fact, no matter how strange this may seem, does not at all cause a child to become braver, more mature or more responsible in a way that can be considered healthy. The end result is simply even more children who have had to miss their childhood.

Having emotionally immature parents means that your childhood will be shortened

One thing we can probably all agree on is that having children alone does not make us parents. Healthy and meaningful motherhood and fatherhood is based on the ability to be present and to cultivate a strong, enriching and true affection. The child should be part of life, not have to walk around with a broken heart full of fear, lack and low self-esteem is

In addition to the basics, such as food and clothing, all children also need something that is also called emotional accessibility. Children need to feel connected to adults, to understand the world and themselves better. If this fails, then everything will collapse. An emotionally immature parent fails to validate the child's feelings. A mother who is only concerned with herself will completely ignore the emotional needs of her children.

On the other hand, it is necessary to indicate that these types of dynamics are much more complex than might initially seem. It can be helpful to distinguish between four types of emotionally immature mothers and fathers.

4 TYPES OF EMOTIONALLY IMMATURE PARENTS

The first type refers to mothers and fathers who exhibit erratic and unpredictable behaviour. These are usually parents who are emotionally unstable. They make promises that they don't keep. One day they can be completely there for their children and the other day they give their children the feeling of being an irritation.

Impulsive parents are parents who act without thinking. They make plans without thinking about the consequences, they pass from one thoughtless mistake to the other, without judging their actions.

Passive parenting is one of the clearest forms of immaturity. Parents like this don't get involved with their children; they are physically present but emotionally and mentally absent. They use a kind of ' laissez-faire ' style to steer their children.

Finally, you have contemptuous parents who give their children the feeling that they are irritation or that they are undesirable. They see raising children as something that is beyond them and something they don't want to have anything to do with.

These four types of emotionally immature parents ensure that childhood is too short, injured and not validated. Children who grow up in this kind of context often experience feelings of abandonment, loneliness, frustrate and anger.

Children who behave like adults: wounds that need to be healed

At the beginning , we also indicated that a child who takes on the role of an adult will not always be stronger, more mature or happier. When you give an eight, ten, or even fifteen year old child full responsibility for caring for himself or for a younger brother or sister, or for making choices that his / her parents should actually make, this leaves a scar on the child who can be the source of a lot of problems in the future.

Five ways to improve your self-confidence

Believing in yourself is not something that happens overnight. Building up confidence takes time and effort.

The feelings of indignation, humiliation and fear that we are subjected to from an early age do not make it any easier. However, it is never too late to start building, even if you are just laying the first stone.

Believe in your own uniqueness

Comparing yourself with others will only cause your confidence to crumble. If you think about it, you will realize that it is actually too absurd for words to compare, after all, we are all different. Instead of wasting time comparing yourself with others and feeling sorry for yourself, you could use your energy much better to take advantage of your abilities, develop your skills, and achieve your goals.

You are not the same as another. You don't have to be this either. What you have is enough because it is what makes you special. Wishing you were different will only undermine your confidence.

Instead, focus inwards and look for your strengths within yourself. You have them, but you have not discovered them because you have been complaining all the time.

Never forget who you are, what you have experienced, and what makes you special. When you know your true self, the person who is hiding under the surface will be reborn.

Leave the pain of the past behind to improve your self-confidence

Is your past really a thing of the past? Not always.

The past is only behind you if you are able to forgive and forget, and if you are able to take advantage of those painful experiences, that is, to learn from them and become stronger. The painful experiences of the past have made you who you are today. Be proud of your scars because they are your strengths.

Sometimes our memories and the betrayal that we experienced in the past are a very heavy burden to bear, and we feel guilty for the mistakes we made. Do not continue to drag this pain with you, choose instead to forgive and move on. Look ahead, live in the present, and focus on your destiny.

Everything that has happened to you is a lesson that you can use to help yourself grow, to create a new level of thinking, and to become stronger and more mature. Don't limit yourself to it. Use your past instead to grow and support your future.

Overcome the fear of leaving your comfort zone

Going outside, your comfort zone is risky. It can, therefore, be pretty scary. But it is certainly the place where you will broaden your horizon and discover a world full of possibilities that you did not know until now. However, to see this place, you must leave your comfort zone.

By taking this first step, even if it is so small, you will get to know yourself better. It will help you to discover your true abilities and to overcome the first real limitation: yourself. After all, your limits are where you place them.

The only way to gain confidence in yourself is to do what you are most afraid of. When you confront these fears, you will see that they are nothing more than insidious products of your mind. And when you confront them, you feel powerful and able to get more out of yourself, to give more of yourself.

You are much more than your past or your labels

Who you are is not determined by your past, your last name, or the labels that are affixed to you.

The people around you may appreciate this, but you are much more than that. You cannot let yourself be defined by this. Of course, it is a part of you, but there are many more things that make your true self complete.

To increase your self-confidence, you need to recognize, find and support yourself. Discovering yourself will trigger a profound transformation. You will start to act differently and be more aware and focused.

This knowledge will also enable you to discover what your vulnerabilities are. Confront your weaknesses with love. Give them a meaning: they are there to show you how you can improve and grow.

Live according to your own values

If you continue to contradict your own values, your mind will slowly die. Your life is yours. You are therefore responsible for it. If you get carried away by what draws you from the outside, and if you are not loyal to yourself, you will no longer be free. You give in and lose your confidence because you let yourself go.

If you find yourself in a situation or relationship that you don't like, remember that it is the result of your decisions. Also remember that you can choose a better path for yourself, even though it seems so impossible to break the pattern.

However, if you look at the situation again and get it through the filter of your own values, you will see how your self-confidence will flourish as a result of your stamina and mental strength. Your values are much stronger than external obligations and social habits. If nobody lives for you, nobody can decide for you. Therefore, revise your values and rediscover yourself.

Our self-confidence will flourish when we take control of our lives, when we sit behind the wheel, instead of in the passenger seat. Making decisions based on what's right for you will help you overcome unavoidable difficulties. This will also help you to improve your confidence.

5 TRAITS OF EMOTIONALLY IMMATURE PEOPLE

There are many myths about the issues of maturity and immaturity. People do not want them to be put in a box or to get a label attached. Each of us is a melting pot in which different forms of consciousness are mixed. We are ignorant and wise, childish and old-fashioned, childish and conscientious. Everything at the same time, although a particular characteristic depends more on the moment than another.

Emotional immature can be defined as a state in which people have not given up their desires or fantasies from childhood. Cravings and fantasies that have to do with the world that revolves around them, or with the reality that adapts to what they want. Similarly, emotional maturity can be defined as a state of strength and moderation that leads to realistic and balanced actions.

More than through an abstract definition, maturity or immaturity comes to light through behavioural characteristics. Here we draw up a list of five traits that are typical of emotionally immature people.

1. Egocentrism

A large part of the maturity of people consists of understanding that the world does not revolve around them. A baby doesn't know that yet. That is why he asks for food at two in the morning and does not care whether this influences his parents' sleep. As he grows, he learns that it is not always possible to get everything he wants and that he lives together with other people who have different needs.

Growing up means escaping this self-centred prison. It means that you lose the illusion that you had as a baby: it is enough to ask for a need or desire to meet. When we give up this fantasy little by little, we simultaneously become aware of an attractive possibility: the adventure of exploring the world of others. If all goes well, we learn to keep our I and to reach you.

2. Difficulty in accepting agreements

A clear sign of immaturity is having difficulty accepting agreements. A child finds it difficult to give up what he wants at that moment to achieve a greater goal in the long term. If we give him candy and we promise him that if he doesn't eat it right away, he'll get another one later, the desire to eat the candy he has in his hand will win.

As they mature, people begin to understand that sacrifice and limitations are necessary to achieve certain things. And that if you make a commitment, or if you make a compromise with someone, this is not a restriction of your freedom, but a condition for functioning better and in the long term.

3. The tendency to blame others

Children assume that they are sent by others who do not act arbitrarily. To a large extent, they become that too, while they are in the process of formation and integration into the culture. While they are small, they think that a mistake automatically leads to guilt. They do not care so much about the damage they have done, but about the punishment or sanction that can be imposed on them.

To grow is to leave this state of sweet irresponsibility. Growing up means understanding that we are the only ones responsible for what we do or do not do. Learning to recognize mistakes and to learn new lessons from them. Know how to repair the damage. Can say sorry.

4. Creating dependency bands

For immature people, others are a means and not an end in themselves. So, as a tool, they think they are, they need them. They don't need others because they love them, but they love others because they need them. That is why they create ties in which there is an enormous dependence.

To establish connections on the basis of freedom, there must be autonomy. However, immature people do not fully understand the concept of autonomy. Sometimes they think that doing what they want comes from autonomous behaviour. But when it comes to accepting the consequences of the actions, they need others to take responsibility.

5. Emotionally immature people handle money irresponsibly

Impulsivity is one of the most striking features of immature people. Impulsivity that is reflected many times in the way they manage their assets, such as money. Therefore, to satisfy their desires, and to do this directly, it is no problem to buy what they don't need, with money that they don't have.

Sometimes they embark on absurd financial adventures. They do not objectively assess the investments and find it difficult to see themselves in the medium and long term. That is why they are often in debt, all just to satisfy impulses.

EMOTIONAL NEGLECT; THAT WHICH WAS NOT THERE

This form of neglect is a phenomenon that is often overlooked because it usually happens silently and invisibly. Unlike physical neglect, of which there are signs such as bruises or malnutrition, emotional neglect is difficult to determine. Emotional neglect is also generally not recognized by the person himself until its symptoms appear in adulthood.

Because as an adult you later receive comparative material, for example, because of your own parenting or you notice that others have had a different upbringing than you, you will discover that you have missed something as a child. That can be a characteristic of emotional neglect. It is about what was not there.

Education and relationships

In children, emotional neglect can occur from birth. Children who were born prematurely or ill and are in the incubator had to miss the first attachment phase with the mother. This can leave an imprint of fear and loneliness in the brain, which the child continues to carry as an adult.

In a later phase of development, emotional neglect has to do with a lack of alignment. A child cannot yet name or place its own emotions. Because the parent can tune into the needs and feelings of the child, the child learns through the parent what emotions it experiences. If this coordination does not take place, the child is emotionally dependent on himself to explain what he or she is experiencing. It often goes wrong here. A child translates the lack of alignment and connection with the parent into an inner experience of 'being wrong', 'not being good enough' or rejection. If this lack of coordination is structural, a foundation consisting of feelings of rejection, uncertainty, shame and self-criticism can arise in the identity of the child.

Emotional neglect also occurs in an adult relationship. For example, your partner cannot tune in to your feelings, even if you indicate them or deny your feelings and cause you to get involved in endless discussions. This eventually leads to isolation within the relationship. You 'starve' emotionally as it were. Research has shown that men often have difficulty with emotions and feelings; they find it confusing, feel responsible for something that they cannot solve, cannot feel well with themselves and generally have more affinity with things than with people. The disadvantage - for both partners - of not being able to share or take emotions and feelings seriously, is that it ultimately overcomes the intimacy between the two partners. What can also happen is that emotional neglect from the past causes you to crave connection, which leads you to choose a partner that does not suit you or is good for you. A sense of loneliness, 'emotional starvation' or lack of real connection has been part of your identity for such a long time that you do not recognize how much you actually lack with the wrong partner. The lack of own identity - knowledge about yourself and knowing what you need -, low self-esteem and the 'starvation' in the emotional area, means that you can later 'cling' to unhealthy forms of attention or love. This can lead to a series of broken relationships and further damage. A sense of loneliness, 'emotional starvation' or lack of real connection has been part of your identity for such a long time that you do not recognize how much you actually lack with the wrong partner. The lack of own identity - knowledge about yourself and knowing what you need -, low self-esteem and the 'starvation' in the emotional area, means that you can later 'cling' to unhealthy forms of attention or love. This can lead to a series of broken relationships and further damage. A sense of loneliness, 'emotional starvation' or lack of real connection has been part of your identity for such a long time that you do not recognize how much you actually lack with the wrong partner. The lack of own identity - knowledge about yourself and knowing what you need -, low self-esteem and the 'starvation' in the emotional area, means that you can later 'cling' to unhealthy forms of attention or love. This can lead to a series of broken relationships and further damage. Low self-esteem and 'starvation' in the emotional area means that you can later 'cling' to unhealthy forms of attention or love. This can lead to a series of broken relationships and further damage. Low self-esteem and 'starvation' in the emotional area means that you can later 'cling' to unhealthy forms of attention or love. This can lead to a series of broken relationships and further damage.

Emotional neglect can take many forms. From a parent who has unrealistically high expectations or does not listen attentively, to debilitating or denying a child's emotional experiences. Making it start to doubt itself. When a parent is not emotionally attuned to a child, but otherwise fulfils the physical needs, a child does not learn to understand their emotions and take them seriously. Knowing and naming what you feel and experience inside is a skill that you should ideally learn from a parent. This needs a child to develop himself emotionally. Self-esteem still develops when your emotions and feelings are taken seriously.

A pitfall of emotional neglect is that you can have the feeling that you actually have no reason to complain. After all, no major injustice or abuse has been done to you. You often think: 'it wasn't that bad', 'others have had it much harder than me' or 'there is something everywhere'. This trivialization of emotional neglect is actually denial. However, the consequences, as described above, are undeniable. That is why it is important to take emotional neglect seriously.

Symptoms of emotional neglect

become insensitive to, or cut off from, your own feelings and needs

feeling that something is missing, but not sure what this is

feeling empty inside

little to no development of talents

easily become overwhelmed or discouraged

have low self-esteem

perfectionism

extremely sensitive to rejection

lack of clarity about expectations of others and expectations for yourself

Education

Most parents meant well or did not know better during their upbringing. They generally did what they could do at the time. In that case, there is no question of malicious intent or psychopathology among the parents. They were previously emotionally immature or emotionally underdeveloped. Some may have experienced emotional neglect as a child themselves and therefore have little to give emotionally.

However, there are parenting styles and characteristics that lend themselves to emotional neglect:

Authoritarian parents

Authoritarian parents want their children to follow the rules and have little inclination or time to listen to the feelings and needs of a child. Adults raised as children by authoritative parents may rebel against authority or become submissive. Especially before the 1960s, the motto regarding upbringing was: "Children can be seen but not heard" and "You can only say something when big people have finished talking ." Education at the time was a matter of teaching children decency and adaptation. The necessity of healthy development of a child's own personality and the importance of being allowed to state boundaries was virtually unknown to the average parent.

Tolerant parents

Tolerant parents have a 'let-it-happen' attitude with regard to raising their child. They leave children emotionally almost entirely to their own devices. Parents can find it civil to give the emotional-mature example; sometimes, they lack the knowledge and skill, energy, interest or patience to discuss with their child how to deal with emotions. Children raised by tolerant parents may have difficulty setting emotional limits and limits for themselves during adulthood. These people can, for example, get stuck in infinite puberty or student age, so that they cannot get to building an adult life with a career or family. They have no sense of responsibility towards others and remain too 'childish' or 'student-friendly'. Or they become over-responsible; they have learned to be too mature for their age since no one else took responsibility for them. As children, these children often have difficulty setting and indicating boundaries to others, which increases their risk of falling prey to people who want to use them for their own interests.

Perfectionist parents

Perfectionist parents tend to believe that their children can always do more, different or better. These are parents who provide criticism and correction instead of guidance. In this way, a child learns that what they do or don't do can always be different or better in the eyes of their parents. Especially when there is not enough positive attention for who they are - without their performance - in return. It is quite possible that the perception afterwards regarding upbringing varies greatly between parents and children. Positive attention may have been given but not felt. Children of such parents can grow up as perfectionists and have unrealistically high expectations of themselves. They internalize a strict inner critic, which results in fears or the feeling of 'never being good enough'.

Absent parents

Absent parents can be absent for various reasons such as death, illness, divorce, overtime or often travelling. Parents can also be emotionally absent and therefore, not know what is going on in their child. They are there, but they do not guide their children emotionally. Children of absent parents ultimately educate themselves to a large extent. If they are the oldest child, they may also raise their younger brothers and sisters. These children are often overly responsible, what they can take with them into their adult lives. These children look like small adults, overloaded with worrying about themselves, others and the world.

It is quite possible that your parents were a combination of the above examples.

Healing with emotional neglect

Healing starts with learning to tune into your own feelings and emotions. By increasing awareness about what you feel and giving yourself permission for these feelings, the process of change begins. Recognizing and naming feelings, she identifies. Being able to identify feelings is a skill that you can learn. Then you learn to accept your feelings and emotions and take them seriously. You have feelings and emotions for a reason because they have a lot to tell you about. There are no 'bad' emotions, but there are effective and less effective ways of dealing with them.

Letting go means that you develop emotionally healthy behaviour.

Patterns of the past concern (in addition to the more 'visible' physical abuse and sexual abuse): the invisible patterns of affective neglect, emotional abuse and / or mental abuse, witnessing this and pedagogical neglect and abuse.

Affective neglect means that you have not received attention, appreciation, acknowledgement, confirmation, comfort and encouragement and that you did not feel that you were allowed to be there and that you were taken seriously and that you felt heard. A child needs and is entitled to these affective aspects. However, not all parents are able to give this to their children.

Emotional abuse is that emotional diet (attention, appreciation, recognition, confirmation, comfort, etc.) does not go from the parent to the child (as it should be), but goes from the child to the parent in the opposite direction. This happens when the child is involved with the parent in one way or another. All marriages of parents of people with (psychological) problems as indicated above are unequal, that is to say, that there is a dominant (er) parent and a subordinate (er) parents. It is usually the subordinate parent with whom the child is involved. A child that has to do with one of its own parents will spare itself and turn away. If a child sees that one of the parents cannot handle it, it is a threat to the child. The child cannot help but the parent. The child can not be a child by taking care of himself and giving it away and by the developing helper role. Later this child, because it seems familiar to him or her, will also want to save and help and care for the partner, and without realizing it he will therefore be attracted to someone who in some way comes across as pathetic, endearing or in need of help. . That is why this child later also enters into an unequal relationship in which one of them takes on a dominant (er) role and the other takes on a subordinate (er) role. History repeats itself, and that goes from one generation to the other. Also, the grandmother and the grandfather from both paternal and maternal side of this child had (very) probably an unequal and unbalanced relationship.

Spiritual abuse concerns all forms of being brought down, not being good (enough), not being good. Spiritual abuse takes place both verbally and verbally.

Pedagogical neglect means that the parents show no interest in school achievements or in the child's interests or activities. Educational abuse means that the child has not been able to make their own education and / or career choice.

The witnessing of physical or verbal violence is just as damaging to a child as being the subject of this violence. Brain research has shown that in a child, the same areas of the brain light up when witnessing physical or verbal violence as when it undergoes physical or verbal violence itself. What an adult can do: make a distinction between the other and himself with regard to the violence. Apparently, a child is not yet (sufficient).

Because emotional abuse is a consequence of effective neglect, these forms always take place together: someone who is emotionally neglected is also emotionally abused and vice versa.

In 98% of cases, if there is effective neglect and emotional abuse, mental abuse also takes place. Scientific research has shown that 40% of current adults have somehow been affected by these forms of child abuse and that half of that 40 % are aware of this and that the other half (therefore 20%) is unaware of it.

In all cases that there is physical abuse or sexual abuse, there is also affective neglect, emotional abuse and mental abuse.

WHAT IS EMOTIONAL ABUSE?

This form of violence cannot be seen from the outside but leaves emotional wounds and scars on the soul. It is difficult to heal these wounds, especially when the abuse took place early in life. Emotional abuse goes unnoticed for a long time; for those who suffer, but also for the outside world. This makes this form of abuse so damaging.

Children and adults

When you grew up under these circumstances, you did not know for a long time that the harmful behaviour of a parent was not normal. After all, the unsafe home environment was 'normal' for you. Because maltreatment is presented as normal behaviour by a parent/confidant, a child starts to believe that. When a child wants to stand up for itself, it is punished or denied by harmful behaviour (characterized by ignoring, humiliation, insult, contempt, ignorance or criticism) of the parent. A child who has disconnected or undermined his own needs learns that it must be 'good' instead of 'real'. This can result in it feeling like a cheater, fake or sneaking, waiting for the lie to come out. This makes the child believe that it is a problem itself. If a child does not have healthy examples, does not learn what is normal or is not allowed to stand up for himself, then it can happen that a child does not learn to build his own identity and healthy life. That can cause many problems later in life.

Not only a parent/guardian can abuse emotionally, but also a partner, child, teacher, employer or colleague. Do you live with the consequences? Such as: always being in conflict, uncertainty, feeling unsafe, inexplicable gloom and not knowing what you want. But also trouble with relationships, fears, addictions, physical complaints, feeling numb and apathy? Then it is possible that you have (had) to deal with emotional abuse.

Through emotional abuse, you get split inside, and you lose part of yourself. In the moments of abuse, you get damaged. The victim of emotional abuse becomes trapped in a web of dishonesty, inability and insecurity, in which self-confidence becomes increasingly weaker.

It may be that a parent, partner or child has an (undiagnosed) personality disorder, such as narcissistic personality disorder, borderline personality disorder, anti-social personality disorder or a theatrical personality disorder. These disorders fall under the cluster B disorders. Machiavellism is not a recognized disorder in the DSM-V but describes the behaviour of many narcissists and psychopaths. Alcoholics can emotionally mistreat, as well as people with non-congenital brain injury, people with low talent or mild intellectual disability. The term KOPP child refers to Children of Parents with Psychiatric Problems. There are various practices within assistance that specialize in assistance for this target group, including this practice. It is not always clear what diagnosis a person has, but the harmful behaviour towards others can be classified as emotional abuse.

It is not the intention of this site to demonize people with a personality disorder or (social) disability. Often - but not always - these people themselves have also been victims of emotional abuse or emotional neglect and therefore have been damaged in childhood. These people are, therefore, often victims and perpetrators themselves. Not everyone who has been a victim of mistreatment passes this on to others. This fact makes it complex. Although victims can feel compassion for damaging the assault, this damage should never be used as an excuse to properly communicate, tolerate, or continue the damaging behaviour to others. The fact remains that the environment suffers considerably as a result. Every assault must take their own responsibility in this. Depending on the degree of self-understanding and motivation for change at the assault, it is possible to treat these people

If you find it difficult to speak of emotional abuse, rename it. For example, an unsafe relationship. Remember that someone manipulates your trust, dependence, affection, naivety, road-numbering qualities or peace-loving nature that falls under the term emotional abuse. To gain insight into the extent of abuse that has happened to you, it helps to write it down. Sometimes the seriousness of what has happened to you only realizes when you see it on paper again.

Subtle

Emotional abuse can be very subtle in the form of manipulation. People who manipulate usually work on your sense of responsibility, guilt or compassion. They themselves are not bothered by that, because they always play the victim when it suits them. We can all be victims of this situation at any time in life. Whether this is in the relationship, within the family or even at work. In such cases, it is especially important that you, as a victim, are able to recognize the situation in which you are trapped. Also that you recognize that the abuser has been able to put all responsibility/blame on you. To free yourself, it is therefore important to, first of all, become aware of the situation in which you find yourself.

Help with emotional abuse

A specialized expert can help you get your energy back, rebuild your identity (again) and increase your confidence so that all those invisible wounds can heal.

CHILDREN OF PARENTS WITH PARANOID PERSONALITY EMOTIONAL PRISONS

The children of parents with paranoid personality exist, although they are invisible to society. They suffer from the consequences of an unorganized attachment, an emotional instability that leaves traces and a very debilitating dysfunctional environment. They are small with a higher risk of mental disorders and who require greater medical-social care together with their families.

People with personality disorders, with schizophrenia, with dissociative disorders, etc. they also fall in love, have children and build their own families. This is clear, but many of them, who do not have sufficient social and family support, result in extreme situations that remain in the shade. We are talking about a problematic dynamic that we are not always aware of.

For example, it often happens that patients with a paranoid personality neglect their treatments and that they are also characterized by a bad relationship with their environment. All this creates situations at very complicated moments, where the children are undoubtedly the most vulnerable link. Therefore, it is necessary to visualize a little more these realities that occur daily in our closest scenarios, where the disease profiles are situations that require our attention and sensitivity.

Living with a person with a paranoid personality

To this day, we still do not know what or why this type of disorder is developing. It is generally assumed that this is the result of this complex triad in which biological, genetic and social factors are added together. That must be said; the paranoid personality is one of the most debilitating psychiatric disorders for a variety of reasons: it affects all aspects of the person, making every person, family, and work relationship very difficult.

Let's look at some functions:

They are profiles that are characterized by permanent distrust. This disorder begins to become apparent in adolescence when they display behaviours of constant suspicion, thinking that others always have bad intentions toward them.

Continuously suspect that they will be misled, betrayed, abandoned ...

Excessive concern for almost every aspect.

They constantly show loyalty and loyalty.

Mismanagement of their emotions are unable to forgive or forget any aspect they regard as an insult, to the point of obsessively storing eternal resentment.

They are hypervigilant. They have always "turned on" their radar for any suspicion, danger, or threat to their person.

In them, that suspicion corresponds to a character who is often cold and hostile. They are people who are always on the defensive.

Children of parents with a paranoid personality

Several studies have been conducted to find out what the impact is of a parent with a paranoid personality in the education of their children. To begin with, it should be noted that the problem in these cases is two-fold. We must not forget that this condition has a genetic weight; that is, there is a clear risk that the prevalence of this disease will be transmitted from one generation to the next.

However, genetics never determines 100% the risk of developing a mental illness, what most determines is undoubtedly our environment and the parenting patterns received. This is where the real problem is no doubt. Now let's see what scientific research tells us about how children of parents with a paranoid personality tend to grow and grow up.

Children of parents with paranoid personality: effects on parenthood and education

At the age of two, children already show a more elusive appearance and less susceptibility to external stimuli.

Uncertain attachment, disorganized and marked by stress, determines that these children exhibit behavioural patterns based on distrust, hyperactivity, fear of abandonment, the constant search for comfort ...

Another common factor that characterizes parents and mothers with a paranoid personality is the emotional and educational incongruity. At times they are very effective, then they show coldness and hostility.

They are inconsistent with the standards, and this generates high stress in the development of the child's brain.

Children of parents with a paranoid personality have a low self-image and a negative self-image.

Emotional restraint because parents have invalidated their emotional and emotional needs from the start.

They usually have very low school performance.

When the child becomes aware of his parent's disease, he usually shows feelings of guilt.

Parents with a paranoid personality often use walls for the socialization of their children. With this, they try to prevent them from being abandoned at a given moment.

During adolescence, It often happens that criminal behaviour is displayed, as well as challenging behaviour, anxiety disorders, depression, etc.

Current interventions

The children of parents with a paranoid personality undoubtedly need a personal psychosocial intervention. Because the effects of an inconsistent and unpredictable family environment are very broad, we cannot stay with the children alone. The intervention must be extended to the entire environment, including parents.

When a couple or a mother with a paranoid personality gives birth, it is necessary to follow psychotherapy based on the improvement of attachment. The mother or father is encouraged to talk about their own childhood experiences and to link these events to their current relationship with their child, allowing them to understand how the unorganized and / or uncertain attachment cycle is perpetuated.

On the other hand, we must also continue to promote adequate psycho-family education, offering adequate support networks. Dynamics such as training in family skills or the need to be consistent in terms of affection, norms, routines and habits are therefore essential goals to achieve in these family centres.

On the other hand, and to conclude, in case the children of parents with a paranoid personality are older, and this problem is already discovered in the school environment, the psychological intervention will be very specific. The child or adolescent will be guided to give him a good sense of self-esteem, to have a positive relationship with their environment, to have them have healthy interests and to equip them with strategies to relieve stress reduce that caused by the mental illness of one of their parents.

They are because we see very complex situations that require concrete and multidisciplinary support.

EFFECTS ON CHILDREN

The development of a child largely depends on the interaction with the parents. That certainly applies in the first years of life. Later the environment will play an increasingly important role.

For a growing child, the loving care and attention of the parent is a basis for developing trust. This allows the child to develop in a safe atmosphere. Moreover, the positive attention of the parent stimulates the child to develop in a balanced emotional, intellectual and physical area.

In the case of child abuse, this security is lacking, and the development of a child comes under severe pressure. It undermines the child's confidence in others. If the child experiences the outside world as hostile or unpredictable, it disrupts his interaction with the children and adults around him. The child seeks the blame for the behaviour of the abusive parent (or another adult) in himself. As a result, he gets a distorted, negative image of himself and his self-confidence gets a big dent.

The extent to which the child's development comes under pressure can vary. The most important factors that determine the effect are:

the seriousness of the violence, neglect or abuse in itself

the age at which it starts

how long it lasts

the presence or absence of support from the environment

the child's personality

the degree of emotional pressure

Consequences during childhood

One of the possible consequences of child abuse in the short term is a physical injury. In extreme cases, with severe physical abuse or neglect, the child may even die as a result. Child abuse also inhibits development, and child abuse can cause all kinds of psychological problems.

Mistreatment, neglect and sexual abuse cause a lot of stress in children so that the so-called stress response system and the part of the brain that controls cognitive and emotional functions (the prefrontal cortex) develop abnormally. The stress response system of children who have been abused, neglected or misused is constantly on the alert and hypersensitive, which means that they constantly respond from a stress response (fight, flight, freeze). The change in the brain can also cause difficulty in making decisions, plans, social behaviour and impulse control. In this context, there is a talk of toxic stress. Scientific research shows that the supportive relationships that children experience early in life can reduce the influence of toxic stress.

In families where child abuse takes place, there can also be parentification (a child who takes care of its parents). The interests of the parent are paramount, which hinders the development of the child. As a result, children have too great a sense of responsibility and difficulty setting limits at a later age.

Consequences in adulthood

The long-term consequences of child abuse are all kinds of psychological problems, including post-traumatic stress disorders and dissociative disorders. Health complaints without apparent physical cause also occur. An adult who has been abused as a child can resort to addiction, self-injury and suicide if the memories of the family history become unbearable.

Approximately one-third of the children who have been abused or neglected, maltreated or neglected as an educator later also his / her own children. There is, therefore, regular intergenerational transfer, but not in a large majority of situations. Intergenerational transfer occurs less frequently if the violence was less threatening and less prolonged if the child does not blame it if fewer negative life events have taken place if the mother has few depressive symptoms. In these situations, the chances are that children can recover and not report child abuse to their own children.

Consequences for society

The insecurity that children experience during their upbringing is an important cause of the behaviour that society experiences as a nuisance and as a threat to safety. Addiction is one of the ways to escape the miserable consequences of child abuse in childhood. This addiction to drugs and alcohol causes a nuisance to the environment. Other social consequences of child abuse are the costs of treatment that victims need.

NEGLECT OF CHILDREN

Child neglect is when the basic needs of a child, such as caring, feeding or caring, are deliberately or unconsciously neglected. The consequences of neglect range from developmental and personality disorders to physical damage.

Playing together and listening to wishes and fears is not taken for granted by many children. According to experts, parents often leave their children too early. If children are neglected, they often not only suffer psychological damage but are also later affected by physical problems.

What does a child need?

For a healthy mental, mental and physical development of a child must be satisfied with its basic needs. Unlike adults, children depend on the support of others to meet their needs. They need reliable, stable and predictable social relationships that give them support, inspiration and care for their personal development. The following basic needs (see also "Maslow's need pyramid") are decisive for the development of a child:

physical needs, such as sleep-wake cycle, food, body care, health care and body contact

Security needs, such as protection against hazards and diseases

Affiliation and love needs, such as: belonging to social communities, emotional closeness and connectedness

Appreciation and validity need, such as unconditional recognition as a valuable person, support in the development of their own individuality, autonomy

Need for stimulation, play and performance, such as encouraging curiosity, supporting experience and exploring the environment, stimulating interest, strengthening intrinsic motivation

Need for self-realization, such as the development of abilities and talents, the pursuit of individual life goals, development of consciousness

What does neglect mean?

Neglect (or neglect) is basically understood to mean the continued or repeated omission of care by caregivers (e.g. parents) who would be necessary to ensure the mental and physical care of a child. It is a form of abuse. Failure to meet the basic needs of a child over a longer period of time can have serious consequences for his or her mental, physical and physical development. Neglect is, for example, when children are insufficiently nourished, cared for, promoted, supervised health care or protected from danger. The rule is that the younger the children, the greater the risk of permanent physical and mental damage.

Neglect occurs in all social strata. Frequently, financial worries, relationship problems or mistreatment in one's own childhood are risk factors that parents or caregivers neglect their own child. Excessive demands and exhaustion often lead to apathy towards the child.

As a rule, there are two forms of neglect - physical and emotional/mental neglect. Since the two forms often can not be clearly separated, mixed forms can also occur. Often affected by neglect are also the sick, disabled and other needy people.

What is meant by physical neglect?

Physical neglect occurs when parents or caregivers do not provide the child with the necessary basic care or not enough. In extreme cases, physical neglect can even lead to death.

Examples of neglecting physical needs include:

Inadequate supply of food and liquid

Inappropriate clothing (e.g. if the child does not wear appropriate seasonal clothing)

Lack of personal hygiene (e.g. if the child always wears soaked diapers)

Irregular and non-age-appropriate bedtime

Inadequate medical or health care (e.g. if the child is very often ill)

No security against everyday dangers (e.g. poisoning, apartment fires, accidents, etc.), lack of supervision

What is meant by mental neglect?

Mental or emotional neglect manifests itself mostly through a careless handling and derogatory care of the child. Emotional neglect is, for example, when:

Children are given too little attention and attention

Children are left alone all the time

Children are not supervised according to their age and are exposed to dangers

Children received no attention and love

Children constantly feeling cold

Children are disregarded

Children hostility is met

Children are constantly shouting

the child constantly condescending criticism and is never praised

Children who are denied social contact with their peers and adults

the child is not supported in making their own experiences

the child is not appreciated

How do you recognize a neglected child?

If a child is neglected, this is usually not recognizable to outsiders. This can be particularly dangerous for babies and toddlers because they can not defend themselves and are helplessly exposed to the abuse. Often a child has been neglected for a long period of time as the consequences become apparent. It is therefore important to know the symptoms and possible "warning signs" of a child in order to recognize the neglect of children at an early stage.

Physical symptoms:

Frequent illness (e.g. respiratory diseases, infections etc.)

underweight

overweight

short stature

Physical aberrations

Delayed motor development

poor posture

allergies

Psychosocial symptoms:

Disturbed social behaviour

Lack of distance or complete withdrawal

Difficult to contact other children or adults

Restricted gaming behaviour

hyperactivity

indifference

sleep disorders

eating disorder

Mental symptoms:

language difficulties

difficulty concentrating

cognitive disorders

learning difficulties

How should one act on suspicion of neglect?

If you suspect that a child in your environment is neglected, you should first keep calm and note the following:

Avoid rash acts. Striking symptoms can also have completely different causes. Try to contact the affected child and offer your help.

If there is suspicion of neglect, seek professional help from the appropriate authorities and, for example, contact a child protection centre. They know what to do and what subsequent steps must be taken!

Rethink a police ad. If the police find insufficient evidence, for neglect, the child can not be guaranteed effective protection. Often the child often has to live in the same environment in case of suspicion and may be exposed to even greater danger after being reported.

How can one avoid neglect?

Parents and carers can learn which symptoms indicate whether a child is at risk, how to proceed in the case of suspicion and which legal framework exists in special parent training and child protection training courses in schools, kindergartens and hoarding.

WHEN CHILDREN SUFFER FROM EMOTIONAL NEGLECT

When we speak of emotional neglect, it never falls on deaf ears, especially when talking about a child. A child is emotionally neglected when its needs are ignored, which in extreme cases, can damage one's psyche and, moreover, damage one's physical health.

The first definition of the word for the neglected verb is: "Do not pay enough attention to anyone, not caring or caring for someone." As soon as a child is emotionally neglected, it feels like abandonment that parents sometimes use Try to balance the satisfaction of its material needs.

Love and affection are essential for the emotional development of a child

In childhood, it is important for a child to feel that their parents are worried about what it takes. Unfortunately, it often happens that they are so focused on the material needs that they completely ignore the emotional ones. Of course, a child also needs material things like clothes, toys; Items that serve his good, etc., but a child also needs signs of love, such as a hug or conversation about his state of mind.

There are some circumstances that can be the root cause of this problem: in many cases, emotional neglect, for example, lack of parent time for the child goes hand in hand. From time to time, parents' long hours do not allow them to take care of their child as much as they would like. By not being able to strengthen their emotional attachment in a common way, they are quickly tempted to consolidate it by other means.

But love and affection are incredibly important to the emotional development of a child so that it grows up happy and mentally healthy: some experts believe that a child needs to have sufficient assurance and affirmation to feel part of the family. Otherwise, the emotional damage that the child suffers could be irreversible.

What are the consequences of the emotional neglect of a child?

The consequences that can result from emotional neglect are even worse in the case of a child. This experience, through which the child can suffer psychological harm and the concomitant lack of love, can become a brand of childhood, which will accompany the child throughout his life. In the following, we will observe some of these consequences:

Difficulties in school: After the family environment, the school is the second most important place where it grows up. If the child does not feel well at home and has problems there, they also become noticeable at school. All of his negative emotions affect his academic performance, his everyday life at school, and his relationships with other children.

Eating Disorders: When we feel bad, it usually affects our eating behaviour immediately. Emotional neglect increases the likelihood that external health will be compromised, and the resulting disorder may need to be treated with psychologist therapy.

Low self-esteem: This may even be one of the most important points to consider. This may not always be the case about a child who is emotionally neglected has typical self-esteem, which decreases gradually more and more. This may also have an impact on the development of his personality and may be expressed through co-dependence, violence or even depression in adulthood.

Depression and anxiety: The emotional damage can manifest in adulthood. Lack of self-confidence or lack of self-confidence can lead to depression and anxiety that complicate everyday life and future interpersonal relationships.

Negative effects on one's future family: Since the emotional neglect affects a child negatively, it is more likely that the affected person makes the same mistakes due to the lack of love for family members of their own established family. Many parents who do not care about the emotional health of their children have also not experienced love from their own parents.

Every child can become the victim of emotional neglect in his or her life, even if it concerns only one phase of life. Any sign of emotional neglect should be treated with a specialist who can help find a way out of this predicament and a solution to the emptiness created by the lack of love.

DEPRESSION IN CHILDHOOD

Depression in childhood exists, even if you know little about it. Depressed children are sad children who cry, who do not laugh, who constantly get angry and do not enjoy life. Children are drowning in grief in their lives. Children whose innocence is clouded by the terrible monster of depression.

Because in the end, yes, there are children who are in deep sadness. Children who can not laugh because their reality does not allow them. It seems unreal because the picture we have of childhood is one of laughing, happy and playing people.

If we see a serious and bent child, then we want to tell him that it should not be sad. We tell him not to cry, but to laugh. That's the first serious mistake.

A depressed child carries on an inner dialogue with himself, which is only rarely visible and explicit. Part of the questions it asks are, "How can I force myself to feel better? Why do people insist that I laugh, play, do not cry and never get angry? I can not stop feeling irritated; why is that? Why is everyone looking so funny at me? Maybe I'm funny, and it's not worth the effort. "

Depression in childhood: asymptomatic depression

Depression in childhood exists, and there are clinical signs that something is not going right inside our little ones. Some of the symptoms are the same as in adults, such as sadness and decreased performance. However, irritability and aggressiveness are much more common in childhood depression. Also occur here more often somatic complaints such as headache, abdominal and muscle pain.

We can also see how darkness stifles the motivation of those affected and their desire to play or engage in various activities. It can also be stated that the child does not eat or sleep properly and often suffers from a general lack of energy.

A child suffering from depression may not be able to focus well or make decisions. It may even have thoughts about death or ideas, plans and suicide attempts.

If you observe five or more of the above symptoms in your offspring, a specialist will likely diagnose depression in childhood.

It is also possible that we notice some motor restlessness in depressed children, which is called agitated depression. This is an atypical depression: the child can not sit still. It seems the chair is burning on his skin. It wrings his hands, goes constantly up and down, drumming with his fingers ...

It seems to have an always full battery. This condition should not be confused with hyperactivity. Therefore, it is always essential for experts to observe all other symptoms that may accompany the diagnosis.

The counterpart to agitated depression can be seen in slow depression. The little one thinks, speaks and moves in slow motion. You can not talk to him, and you have to repeat all the questions you ask him. His themes are always the same, and he remains silent for long periods of time.

Another clue maybe when the child has very low self-esteem. The child may think that it is worthless and inherently flawed. It may even magnify the mistakes in his perception.

But you should always keep in mind that certain states of apathy, aversion or sadness are completely normal.

In fact, we should consider the apathy or sadness of a child with caution. We often insist on telling them to be happy without understanding what makes them feel so uncomfortable. That is, it conveys that sadness, frustration and anger are not normal, that they are useless emotions.

Let's think about what that implies for a child or a teenager. Is not it normal to be sad about a loss? Do not we all feel annoyed at some point? Are not these emotional states useful for putting things to work?

10 IDEAS TO HELP A DEPRESSED CHILD FEEL BETTER

Lead by example: Smile, show good humour, enjoy your free time and holidays, think aloud in a sensitive way, etc.

Help the child to have fun and feel good: Plan pleasant and fun activities, invite his friends home, surprise them with innovative and attractive plans, pay attention to their successes, keep their preferences in mind.

Protect It from Unnecessary Suffering: Take care of your health (vaccinations, hygiene, sleeping habits, food, and so on), prepare it for stressful situations (for example, the beginning of a school year or the death of a family member).

Promote a harmonious environment within the family and at home: express your love with words and deeds; Avoid having parents talk in their presence.

Educate them with affection and coherence: behave in accordance with the environment, set up appropriate rules of conduct and demand their cooperation. Be understanding and flexible, cooperate with your school.

Promote their qualities, hobbies and interests: register with the sports club, awaken their interest in reading, music, theatre, film, collecting, crafts, etc. Encourage them to try enriching experiences such as new flavours, sports or games.

Train them to deal with frustration: Do not respond to their irrational demands. Ignore her spirited theatre. Teach them to wait for their turn. Delay the fulfilment of your demands step by step. Get them to share their toys and possessions.

Make them responsible, not guilty: appreciate the effort of their learning and not their scores. Set realistic goals and congratulate them accordingly. "Congratulations on your grades!" Is better than I "want the next time see only ones! "

Form a rational way of thinking: Avoid labels and absolutist language like "You're bad. You never do it right. " Instead of simplifying the solution, make them think about it. Question: "What could we do to solve this? And what else? "Talk to them, reject their irrational ideas and ideas.

Strengthen your autonomy: Teach them fundamental skills, such as washing or dressing, cooking, or how to handle their money. Give them the opportunity to practice. Help them with everything, if necessary, but do not solve their problems for them. Allow them to take part in the decision-making process bit by bit.

Nevertheless, if we observe any of the above symptoms for a continuous-time, then we should contact a specialist to examine the child. They will work together on the aspects described above.

And that will illuminate the fantastic smile that every child should show on his face and in his heart.

The emotional health of children is not something that just magically occurs. It is something that you have to cultivate.

THE CONSEQUENCES OF EMOTIONAL NEGLECT IN CHILDHOOD

The most important characteristic of a person is the ability to form and maintain relationships with other people. These relationships are absolutely necessary for each of us to survive, to learn, to work, to love, and to reproduce.

Interpersonal relationships take many forms, but the most intense, pleasant and painful are relationships with friends, family, and loved ones. Within this small inner circle of intimate relationships, we are bound together by "sentimental kitt" - bound by love.

The ability to form and maintain relationships through this "feeling" is different for each individual. Some people seem to be naturally capable of being able to love. They form many intimate and loving relationships and enjoy them. Others are not so happy. They have no inclination to form intimate relationships, and have little pleasure in being close to or close to others. They have few, if not less, friendships, if anything, less sense of humor within the family. In extreme cases, it happens that an individual has no perfect emotional connection with anyone at all. They are self-sufficient, unapproachable or even show classic psychiatric signs of schizophrenia or autism.

The ability and desire to create emotional connections are related to the organization and functioning of parts of the human brain. Just as the brain allows us to taste, see, smell, think, speak and move, the organ that allows us to love - or not. There is a systems in the human brain that allow us to build and maintain emotional connections occur during childhood and the early years of life. The experiences during this early vulnerable phase of life decisively shape the ability to form intimate and healthy emotional bonds. Compassion, tenderness, sharing, mastering one's own aggression, love ability, and a host of other characteristics of a healthy,

Frequently asked questions

What is love attachment?

Depends on. The word "bonding" is used regularly by professionals in psychotherapy, child development and child protection, but has a slightly different meaning in these different contexts. First of all, we make people many types of bonds. A bond is a connection between peope. In infant development, "attachment" refers to a specific binding that is characterized by the unique properties of the particular band that forms in maternal-infant or primary caregiver-infant relationships. The love bond has several key elements:

she is a lasting emotional relationship with a special person;

the relationship provides security, well-being, soothing and pleasure;

the loss or danger of losing this person causes intense suffering.

This particular form of relationship is best represented by the mother-child relationship. In our research into this particular relationship, we found out how important it can be for the child's future development. Many scientists and therapists consider the mother-child relationship to be the working model for all subsequent relationships that the child will develop. A stable and healthy love affair with the primary caregiver appears to be associated with a high probability of healthy relationships, while a weak love affair with the mother or primary caregiver appears to be associated with numerous emotional and behavioral problems later in life.

In clinical psychology, attachment is widely used to generally refer to the ability to enter into relationships. In the context of this publication, attachment capacity generally refers to the ability to enter and maintain emotional relationships, while attachment is related to the nature and depth of the relationship. For example, a child may have "insecure" or "safe" attachment.

What is Bonding or Bonding?

Simply put bonding is the process of making a love bond iS attachment. Just as bonding is the expression one uses when one individual attaches to another, this bond design uses our sentimental kink to connect with one another. Bonding therefore involves a series of behaviors that help us to bond with our emotions.

Are bonding and attachment genetically determined?

The biological ability to make and form bonds is most likely genetically determined. The survival instinct is fundamental in all species. Infants are vulnerable and their survival depends on a caring adult. Against the background of this primary dependence and the maternal response to this dependency, a relationship develops. Survival depends on this love bond.

A physically and emotionally healthy mother will be attracted to her infant - she will have a bodily longing to smell, hug, rock, "gu-gu", and look at her baby. The infant, on the other hand, responds by nestling, babbling, smiling, sucking, and stapling. In most cases, the mother's behavior provides pleasure, reassurance, and nutrition to the infant, and the infant's behavior gives the mother pleasure and contentment. It is in this cycle of mutual positive feedback, this mother-baby dance, that attachment develops.

Thus, despite the genetic ability to bind and love, genetic potential is shaped by the nature, quantity, pattern, and intensity of early childhood experiences. Without predictable, attentive, nourishing, and sensible care, the infant will not live up to its capacity for normal attachment and love. The brain functions responsible for healthy emotional relationships will not develop optimally without the right experiences at the right time in life.

What are experiences of bonding?

Experiences of bonding design include hugging, rocking, singing, feeding, watching, kissing, and other nourishing behaviors that are needed to care for infants and toddlers. Decisive factors include time (in childhood, quantity counts!), Direct interaction, eye contact, physical closeness, touch, and other primary sensory experiences such as smell, sound, and taste. Scientists consider positive body contact (eg, pushing, hugging, and rocking) to be the most important factor in building love bondage. It should come as no surprise that hugging, watching, smiling, kissing, singing and laughing trigger specific neurochemical activities in the brain. These neurochemical activities in turn lead to the normal organization of the brain regions,

One of the most important relationship in a child's life is attachment to their first caregiver, ideally to the mother. This is because this first relationship represents the biological and emotional 'model' for all future relationships. A healthy love bond with the mother, built on repeated bonding experiences during infancy, provides a solid foundation for future healthy relationships. In contrast, problems with attachment and love can lead to a fragile biological and emotional basis for future relationships.

When are these time windows?

Timing is everything. Experiences of attachment design lead to healthy attachment and healthy love attachments when they develop during the first years of life. During the process of first three years of life, the human brain develops 90 percent of its final size and forms most of the systems and structures responsible for all future emotional, behavioral, social and physiological functions for the rest of life. There are crucial periods during which bonding experiences must occur in order for the brain regions responsible for attachment to develop normally. These crucial periods seem to be in the first year of life and depend on the ability of the infant and the caregiver to develop a positive interactive relationship.

What happens if this time window is missed?

The effects of impaired attachment experience in early childhood are different. Severe emotional neglect in early childhood can be devastating. Children without touch, stimulation and care can literally lose the ability to make meaningful relationships for the rest of their lives. Fortunately, most children do not suffer such severe neglect. However, there are many millions of children whose bonding and attachment is impaired during early childhood. The resulting problems can range from mild discomfort in dealing with people to serious social and emotional problems. In general, the severity of the problem depends on how early in life,

Very little is known about the ability to replace or cure underdeveloped or poorly organized attachment and love ability through later life experiences. Clinical trials and a variety of studies suggest that recovery may be taking place, but it is a long, difficult and frustrating process for families and children. It can take many years of hard work to repair the damage of just a few months of neglect during infancy.

Are there classifications for bindings?

Similar to size or weight, individual attachment skills vary continuously. However, when trying to study the scale of attachments, scientists have divided the continuum into four attachment categories: safe, uncertain-reluctant, uncertain-avoidant, and uncertain-disoriented. Securely bound children feel a consistent, attentive and supportive relationship with their mother, even in times of considerable stress. Uncertainly bound children feel inconsistent, punitive, indifferent feelings from their caregiver and feel threatened in times of stress.

In short, the mother and child are observed in a series of "situations": mother (or father) and child alone in a playroom; a stranger comes into the room; Mother leaves the child alone with the stranger who plays with the baby and tries to console it; Mother comes back and comforts baby; foreign person leaves the room; Mother leaves baby completely alone; stranger enters and comforts the baby; Mother comes back and tries to comfort and deal with the infant. The behavior during each of these situations is monitored and evaluated.

What other factors influence attachment behaviour and love attachment?

Any factor that interferes with the bonding experience can also disrupt the development of the ability to love. When the interactive, mutual "dance" between caregiver and baby is disturbed or impeded, bonding experiences can hardly be sustained. Disorders can be caused by primary problems of the infant, the caregiver, the environment or the "mating" between the infant and caregiver.

Infant:

The personality or temperament of the child influences the bond development. If a baby is difficult to calm, irritable and unresponsive compared to a quiet, self-satisfied child, he will have more difficulty in establishing a secure bond. The child's ability to participate in the maternal-infant interaction may be affected by medical conditions such as premature birth, birth defects, or illness.

Caregiver:

Caregiver behaviour may interfere with bond development. Critical, rejecting, meddling parents tend to have children who avoid emotional closeness. Abusive parents tend to have children who feel uncomfortable and withdraw when they are near. The mother may not be indifferent to the child due to birth depression, medication abuse, overpowering personal problems, or other factors that interfere with her ability to be reliable and supportive to the child.

Surroundings:

A major obstacle to a healthy love bond is fear. If an infant suffers from pain, debilitating threat, or chaotic environment, it will be difficult for him to participate in an even supportive relationship. Infants or children from domestic violence, refugees from social violence or war zones are prone to attachment problems.

Match:

Matching the temperament and abilities of the infant and mother is crucial. Some carers can get along with a quiet baby but are overwhelmed with a cranky baby. The process of mutual attention, reading one's non-verbal signals and responding accordingly, is essential to foster the development of bonds that engages in healthy love relationships. Sometimes the style of communication and reaction that a mother is used to form one of her other children does not fit into her current infant. The mutual frustration of being "unsynchronized" can affect the bond development.

How do abuse and neglect affect attachment?

There are three main aspects that have been observed in families with abuse and neglect. The most common effect is that maltreated children are rejected in principle. Children who are rejected by their parents have numerous problems (see below), including the difficulty of developing emotional closeness. In abuse families, this rejection and abuse continue mostly across generations. The negligent parents were also neglected as a child. They pass on how they were treated by their parents. Another aspect is "parenting" the child. This can take many forms. A common form is seen when a young, immature girl becomes a single mother. The child is treated as a playmate and very early as a friend. You often hear such young mothers call their four-year-old "my best friend" or "my little man". In other cases, adults are so immature and uninformed about children that they treat their children as adults - or even as a spouse. As a result, their children can participate less in activities with other "immature" children. This misjudgment of maturity often disturbs the development of friendships within one's own age group. The third common aspect is the transgenerational nature of attachment problems. As a result, their children can participate less in activities with other "immature" children. This misjudgment of maturity often disturbs the development of friendships within one's own age group. The third common aspect is the transgenerational nature of attachment problems. As a result, their children can participate less in activities with other "immature" children. This misjudgment of maturity often disturbs the development of friendships within one's own age group. The third common aspect is the transgenerational nature of attachment problems.

It is also very important to note that previously secure bonds can suddenly change as a result of abuse and neglect. The child's perception of a consistent and nourishing world is no longer compatible with its new reality. For example, a child may lose their positive ideas of adults as a result of physical abuse by a babysitter.

Are attachment problems always consequences of abuse?

No, in fact, most attachment problems are more likely due to parents' ignorance of a child's development than to abuse. Many parents are not aware of the crucial importance of their experiences during the first three years of life. This would improve if there were more public information and political support in this area. Currently, this ignorance is so very comon that it is estimated that one in three children has an avoiding, ambivalent or reluctant attachment to their caregiver. Despite this insecure attachment, they can relate and hold relationships - but not with the ease of others.

What specific problems can be expected in maltreated children with attachment problems?

The specific problems that can be observed depending on the intensiity, nature, duration and timing of abuse and neglect .

Some children will have obvious and profound problems; others have more subtle problems that are not at all connected with neglect at an early stage of life. Sometimes these children seem unaffected by their experiences. However, it is important not to forget why you work with the children and that you have been exposed to horrible events. There are some pointers that experienced therapists pay attention to when working with such children.

Developmental delays:

Children who have experienced emotional neglect in their early childhood often show developmental delays in various areas. The bond between the toddler and the caregiver is the most important prerequisite to develop physically, mentally and mentally. In this primary context, children learn a language, social behaviour, and a host of other essential behaviours for healthy development. A lack of reliable and rich experiences in early childhood can lead to delays in motor, language, social, and cognitive development.

Eat:

Strange eating habits are common, especially in children with severe neglect and attachment problems. They hoard food, hide it in their room, eat as if there is no food soon, even if they had a dependable diet for years. You have growth problems, vomit, have difficulty swallowing or in later life strange eating habits, such as anorexia nervosa (anorexia).

Stress reduction behaviour:

These children use very primitive, immature and bizarre stress reduction behaviours. They chew on themselves, bumping their heads, rocking, singing, scratching or cutting themselves. These symptoms increase in phases of suffering or anxiety.

Emotional behaviour:

A variety of emotional problems are common in such children, including depressive and phobic symptoms. Frequently, indiscriminate attachment. All children yearn for safety. With the unconscious knowledge that affection is important for survival, children seek attachment - any attachment - for their own safety. Lay people may think that abused and neglected children "love" and embrace strangers. However, children do not cultivate deep emotional ties with relatively unknown persons; rather, these "love testimonies" are actually forms of seeking security. Psychologists are worried because these behaviours add to the confusion of the abused child with regard to closeness and contradict normal social behaviour.

Inappropriate imitation:

Children mimic adult behaviour - even abuse. They learn that abuse is the "right" way to deal with other people. As you can easily see, this easily causes problems in their social contacts with adults and other children. Children who have been sexually abused are at greater risk for future ill-treatment. Men who have been sexually abused may themselves become sexual offenders.

Aggression:

One of the main problems with these children is aggression and cruelty. This is related to two primary problems of neglected children: (1) lack of compassion, (2) poor control of their impulses. The power to "emotionally" understand the impact of their behaviour on others is impaired in these children. They really do not understand and feel like it is for others when they say or do something painful. These kids often feel compelled to hit each other and hurt others - typically someone weaker than them. They will hurt animals, peers, siblings and smaller children.. The most disturbing thing about this aggressiveness is that it is usually accompanied by a distanced, cold lack of compassion.

How can I help?

Take care of these children:

These children must be held, cradled and caressed. Be there for them, take care of them and love children with attachment problems. Keep in mind that many of these infants have already been linked to pain, agony or sexual abuse. Watch carefully how they react - get involved in the reactions to your care and act accordingly. Give them a variety of compensatory experiences that should have taken place in their early childhood - but when you do, the child's brain is much harder to influence. That's why it takes a lot more bonding experiences to develop love ties.

Try to understand the behaviour before punishing or taking any other action:

The more you learn about attachment, attachment problems, normal and abnormal development, the better you can develop constructive and social behaviour. Information about these issues can prevent you from misunderstanding the child's behaviour. For example, when these children hoard food, this should not be considered as "stealing," but as a frequent and predictable result of unsatisfied hunger during early childhood. Responding to this problem (or many others) with penalties will not help the child to mature. In fact, punishment can exacerbate the child's insecurity, his suffering, and his tendency to hoard food. Many behaviours of these children are confusing and unsettling for the caregivers. But you can get help from experts,

Serve these children according to their emotional age:

Neglected and Abused children are often emotionally and socially left behind. And every time they are frustrated or anxious, they suffer a relapse. This means that at any one time, a ten-year-old can be as emotional as a two-year-old. Despite our desire that they behave "according to age" and despite our admonitions, they are not capable of doing so. These are the moments in which we have to behave towards them, as it is their emotional level. When they are in tears, frustrated, overwhelmed (emotionally biennial) mother them as if they were at this age. Use calming nonverbal attention. Hold her. Weigh it. Sing quietly. Such a situation is not the right moment

Be consistent, predictable and repetitive:

Abused children with attachment problems are sensitive to changes in the daily routine, transitions, surprises, chaotic social and generally new situations. Busy and unique social situations will overtax you, even if they are pleasant! Birthday parties, sleep too long, holidays, family outings, the beginning of the school year and the end of the school year - all these things can confuse these children. Therefore, anything that can be done to be consistent, predictable, and repetitive is very important for those children to feel safe. If they feel safe, they can benefit from the caring and enriching emotional and social experiences you provide them. If they are anxious, they can not do it in the same way.

Live and teach appropriate social behaviour (be a role model):

Many neglected and abused children do not know how to deal with other people. One of the ways to teach them is to make it happen to them - and then tell the child what you do and why. Make a game of playing the announcer: "I go to the sink to wash my hands before eating, because ..." or "I'll take the soap and soap myself in here and ...". Children see, hear and imitate.

In addition to this past life, you can "train" battered children while playing with other children. Use a similar game as an approach: "Well, if you take that away, you're probably going to be pretty angry. So, if you want them to enjoy this game ... "By playing smoother with other kids, they will develop improved self-esteem and confidence. In time, success with other children will make the child socially skilful and less aggressive. Maltreated children are often messy because of their delayed socialization. When the child is teased for his clothes or appearance, it helps to provide "cool" clothing and better hygiene.

An area where these children have problems is to dose physical contact appropriately. You do not know when to hug someone, how close you should stand when to build eye contact, and when to break off when the time is right to drill your nose or touch the genitals.

Ironically, children with attachment problems often take the initiative to contact the body with strangers (hugging, holding hands, sitting on their lap). Adults misunderstand this as an expression of love. That's not it. It is best understood as a submission gesture, and it is socially inappropriate. It is very important how adults handle such inappropriate body contacts. We should not refuse to embrace the child and teach him the right behaviour. We can gently guide the child to deal differently with adults and other children ("Why do not you sit over there?"). It is important to make these lessons clear with as few words as possible. You do not need to be commanding - rely on non-verbal signals. It is also important to explain in a way

Listen to these children and talk to them:

It is very pleasant just to stop, to sit together with these children, to listen to them and to play with them. When you are calm and responding to them, you will soon discover that they are showing you and telling you what is really in them. As simple as it sound, it is very difficult for an adult to stop, stop, think about the time and the next task and really relax with a child at that moment. Practice it. You will be surprised by the results. These children will feel that you are only there for them. You will feel how much you like her.

It is during these moments that you best reach and influence these children. It is an excellent moment to teach children about their different feelings. Regardless of the activity, it is important to observe the following principles: (1) all feelings are alright - sad, happy, angry and so on; (2) Teach the child healthy choices about how to behave when he is sad, happy or angry; (3) Begin to explore how other people feel and how they express their feelings - "What do you think Bob feels when you push him?" (4) If you notice that the child is clearly happy, sad, or angry, ask it how it feels. Help him to find words for his feelings.

Set realistic expectations for these children:

Abused and neglected children have so much to overcome. And some of them will not overcome all their problems. Expectations should be reduced to a Romanian orphan girl who was adopted at the age of five after spending her first years of life without any sentimental nourishment. It was robbed of some of its potentials, but not all. We do not know how to predict the potential in a vacuum, but we do know how to grasp the emotional, behavioural, social and physical strengths and weaknesses of a child. An empathic evaluation by a gifted psychologist can be very useful to find out at the beginning in which areas a child is gifted and on which the progress will be slower.

Be patient with the progress of the child and with yourself:

Progress will be slow. Slow progress will frustrate you, and many adoptive parents feel inadequate, as all the love, time, and effort they dedicate to their child seems to have no effect. But they have an effect. Do not be hard on yourself. Many loving, gifted and competent parents have been inundated by the needs of a neglected and abused child they have accepted.

Take care of yourself:

Worrying about maltreated children can exhaust and discourage. You can not give these children the consistent, predictable, enriching and nourishing care they need when exhausted. Make sure you get peace and support. A nursing break can be crucial. Take the help of friends, family and community. You will not be able to help your child if you are depressed, angry, overwhelmed exhausted, or over-sensitive.

Use other resources:

Many communities have self-help groups for adoptive and foster families. Experts with experience with attachment problems and abused children can help a lot. They will need help. Do not forget: the sooner and more decisively the mediation, the better. Children are most malleable at a young age, and the older they get, the harder the change is.

5 characteristics of emotionally immature people

There are many opinions about when a person shows maturity and immaturity. We humans do not like being put in drawers or putting a stamp on us. Each of us is like a pot in which different forms of consciousness are mixed together. We are ignorant and wise, a child and an old man, childish and conscientious at the same time , although depending on the moment one of the qualities shows itself more than the other.

Emotional immaturity could be defined as a quality that still holds man to the desires or fantasies of childhood . Desires and fantasies related to the idea that the world revolves around itself or, in other words, that reality can be adapted to its own ideas. Conversely, we could describe the emotional maturity as a state of strength and moderation that leads to a realistic and balanced action.

But more than an abstract definition makes maturity or immaturity visible in behavior. Below, we want to introduce you to five characteristics that are characteristic of emotionally immature humans.

1. They are egocentric people

Much of the human maturation process is to understand that the world is not just about one's own person. Of course, a baby does not know that yet. That's why it screams to be fed in the middle of the night, and it does not matter if that bothers his parents' night's sleep. The older the child gets, the more it learns to realize that it does not always get what it wants, and that it lives on this planet with other people who have their own needs.

To mature means to escape the ego prison. It means losing that hope that life could be like a baby's. Namely, that it is enough just to ask for the fulfillment of a need or desire . As we begin to ignore this idea, we become aware of what else life holds for us: numerous adventures and discoveries. At best, we learn to put the ego off and on and sometimes put it in the foreground while maintaining a healthy balance.

2. They barely fulfill their obligations

A clear indication of a person's immaturity is its difficulty in meeting obligations. It is hard for a child to give up something in order to achieve a greater goal in the long term. If we give it a sweetie and promise it that we will give it one more, if it does not eat it now, the desire to eat the candy in his hand will be even greater.

In the process of maturing, the child will understand that sacrificing and taking back time is necessary in order to reach his goal . It will also understand that it is not an incision into his freedom to fulfill one's obligation or to put another person's needs above his own, but a prerequisite for better orientation in the long term.

3. You have a habit of blaming others

Children see themselves as beings led by others who do not act according to their will. For the most part they are, too, which is why they still have to find their place in society and still have to achieve emotional maturity. At a young age, they believe that a mistake inevitably leads to guilt. What harm they do is not so important to them, but more the punishment or other unpleasant consequences that go with it.

Tire means leaving this state of sweet irresponsibility. Tire means slowly understanding that we are the only ones responsible for our actions or our passivity. To learn that we have to admit mistakes and learn something new from them. To know how to fix the damage and apologize.

4. They make themselves dependent on others

For immature persons, other people are the means to an end and never the purpose itself. Because of this, they tend to be heavily dependent on others.

Autonomy is required to create freedom-based attachments . However, emotionally immature people do not understand much of the concept of autonomy. Sometimes they think that it is like acting autonomously to do what they want. But when it comes to bearing the consequences for their actions, they need others to be able to reject the responsibility.

5. You can not handle money

Impulsive behavior is one of the most distinctive features of immature persons. An impulsive behavior that often manifests itself in the way they use their means, especially money. To fulfill their wishes quickly, they often buy useless money they do not yet have.

Now and then they venture crazy financial adventures. They do not value the investments objectively and can hardly plan in the medium and long term. Therefore, they often have debts, and only because they always have to live their whims.

Promote Emotional Development in Children: From the confusion of emotions

Everybody knows this phrase: it usually comes from the back seat of the car, about 15 minutes after the start of the ride, and is repeated in any interval that gets shorter and shorter as the ride progresses Parents are usually (understandably) annoyed by this and share this with the source of the anger as clearly as unsuccessfully: "You are annoying!" or "Stop annoying!"

Emotions are the key to the child

If we want to find out what's happening here and - at least as interestingly - how we can change that, we need to ask ourselves what the situation looks like from the child's point of view.

Specifically, how the child feels right now . Because feelings are the reason why people do or do something.

In the example described above, the case seems to be clear: "The child is boring!" And yes, you are right, the child is boring, but you can also say: the child does not want to annoy or annoy the parents It is not intentional or malicious, but a sense of the child that is uncomfortable with itself and that often can not properly classify it.

So it tries to eliminate this unpleasant feeling, which is more or less conscious to him depending on his age - just by asking "When will we be there soon?". This also works for a moment, because after all, there is a short 'conversation' with mom or dad, which breaks the boredom, however, only for a tiny moment.

How it goes on, we have seen at the beginning. Result: Parents and children are at the end of their nerves, the mood is below zero and both 'parties' wonder if the other side is also nice and easy to maintain ... But it is also different and more enjoyable for both sides , in addition to promoting development for the child:

This allows parents to promote emotional development in children

Reflect feelings of children

Just let the child know what you feel about him, what you believe or feel, just how it feels. So in our example: "You're bored." But maybe also: "You are already very excited, you're looking forward to a great doll." or "You're worried about that ...", "You're afraid of that ...".

This sounds strange, but it helps the child to sort and process his own feelings. After all, the children do not come into the world with the knowledge that there is everything for feelings and how they feel.

Incidentally, this is also one of the reason why small children often have "abdominal pain", no matter where it hurts and how they feel in detail. You must first learn that the rumbling in the abdomen is excitement and the pressure on the chest scares. In many cases this is enough to process a feeling: we accept the feeling as it is and it dissolves.

So you do not always need a solid solution or action. Incidentally, no one can manage to always shake a suitable solution from the sleeve. Since parents should not put pressure.

Safe bonding for optimal emotional development

"Does my child even understand that when I talk to him like this?", You might be wondering now. Well, it has been found that if mothers of infants (!) Could adequately address the emotional states of their baby, for example, "Oh Does your tummy hurt? " "Yes, are you happy, sweetheart, bunny (or what kind of animal you prefer ...)", then a secure bond could be predicted.Secure bonding is something like basic trust and a major protection factor for mental health, even though the babies are proven Do not understand literally what the mother says, it has a positive effect on the child.

From the beginning, children have different feelings. By "mirroring" the child's feelings, we help the child perceive, distinguish, and verbalize their own feelings.

It also sets the foundation for the child to learn to control its emotions when it makes sense. For example, you do not always get tantrums when something does not go your way.

Emotional competence wants to be trained

At the same time, however, when dealing with the emotions, certain brain cells are also trained, which in the first place enable us to develop compassion. We all have these so-called mirror neurons at birth, but they still have to be trained, otherwise they will disappear. The mirror neurons not only make it possible to empathize with other people, they are also the prerequisite for learning by observing others, thus imitating them.

Parents are role models in terms of feelings

Even dealing with feelings, children look from the parents. Because: What the parents do, can not be wrong. Parents thus influence the behavior of their children very strongly by what they show them. How do you go? B. with disappointment or dissatisfaction? Of course you can get angry, that's completely normal, but how should parents react to it when their child has a temper tantrum?

Take children's feelings seriously to promote emotional development

No matter what the feeling is and whether the parents can feel the emotion or feel very different in the place of the child, parents should always accept the child's feeling as it is. There is no right or wrong in feeling.

And feelings can not be talked out or talked about. Did you ever say something like "You do not have to be afraid" or "You do not have to be sad", "Oh well, well then it's good!" Here's a magical notion that we're going through This will, however, in most cases not work ... Feelings are just there and we have to accept them first, anything else would be a reaction like a little kid hands down Eyes shut and says, "I'm not there!"

Parents do not have to accept everything the child does

This difference between feelings and behavior is very crucial! So parents can certainly understand that a kid is jealous of the new sibling, who "steals so much time away from mom." However, of course, one can not approve if it pinches the baby. Likewise, we can accept that a child loved playing with the new friend and forgetting about it because it was so intriguing. But that does not mean that we find his lateness okay.

Take a look at the children

So that parents can understand their child, they should first find out what the world looks like from his point of view. This opens up much that at first seems odd, puzzling and incomprehensible to parents. Children have a different way of thinking than adults.

Young children sometimes rhyme something that adults do not necessarily come by. The younger they are, the more they believe everything in the world happens to them. That is why children, even if they do not say so, often believe that their parents have separated because they are 'naughty, stupid, unlovable'.

This egocentric view of the world has nothing to do with overconfidence, but is developmental. Only gradually children learn to empathize with other people. Parents can encourage children to think about what someone else might feel like, in a story, a storybook, a movie, or playing with hand puppets, playing pieces, dolls, or dressing up. Even so, they promote the emotional development of their children.

15 DELICIOUS THINGS YOU RECOGNIZE WHEN YOU ARE EMOTIONALLY MATURE

Nope: being emotionally mature has nothing to do with age and phase of life. A 50-year-old can still identify as a toddler, and an adolescent can sometimes have wiser thoughts than an 80-year-old. Emotional maturity is about how you approach the world, and the world in turn. And you recognize that by the following things:

You are self-aware

And so you know what you are doing, and why. Not always, and you really blunder once or just say the wrong thing at the wrong time, but then you know that about yourself and you think about that for a moment. And try to do it better next time. You are able to look at yourself through someone else's eyes, thus observing, and you can distance yourself from your own thoughts, emotions and actions in time. As a kind of filter, with which you keep things as neutral as possible. You know your strengths and your weaknesses, and you do it as well as you can.

You have self-control

Emotional outbursts or other 'urges' such as gossip or other awkward ugliness are not strange to you, but you feel them coming, and then you try to suppress them. And that is fine because whoever gives in to every tendency is not to be worried about his or her environment, is it? And that makes the whole difference in your case. Of course, you sometimes get angry, but you stay calm and do not immediately slam doors or speak in toxic tongues. No, your triumph is in calmness, keep your distance and then handle everything nicely. Secret tip: and emotionally immature people can deal with that particularly badly. It only makes it more fun.

You are responsible

That is why you have abandoned the idea that things or people "happen" to you, and you stand in the middle of the playing field that is life. Whether it is your work or your relationships: you have long understood that there is such a thing as an action-reaction, and you take responsibility for that. If you get caught up in a conflict (whatever happens to you), you will look for your own role, but you will not be afraid of saying goodbye if necessary. You do not live passively but are able to change a situation if it requires it.

You are modest

And COME once again at this time, that is why it is so delicious. You are not humble, but you know what gratitude and modesty are worth and you act accordingly. As far as you are concerned, it is not necessary for you to jump on a table to share your own violence with the world, that you are great can also take shape in silence and is much more powerful too, thank you!

You have self-knowledge

Because you know very well that you yourself have such construction errors, you can respond kindly and empathically to someone else's. So there is no need to verbally drop someone off to the ground for his or her shortcomings (let alone behind his or her back): you prefer to spend your time improving yourself. And more people should do that, let's just say.

You are grateful

Gratitude is the key to happiness, and you already know that. And so you focus your attention not on the negative but on all the wonderful people you have around you, the fact that you have a house and food, that you experience everything on a daily basis and that you experience life itself. That is not a saint-bean tone, that is dealing consciously and kindly with your existence. And with that of others.

You know what compassion is.

An adult person cannot help but wish for someone else and will want to help that person if possible. You are more aware than others of the principle of 'interconnection', which means that all people are connected. Your energy is the same as other people's energy, so you are open to volunteering or other ways to help others. And you don't need applause for that; it's actually normal for you.

You focus on others

For you, no endless monologues about yourself, your child, your husband or all your self-centred stuff: you focus on harmony and universal knowledge that we are all together. Jealousy is strange to you, and you grant others their success - even if that success was or was your dream. Exaggerated self-promotion, envy or ignoring others in their success is typical behaviour of less mature fellow human beings. But that doesn't really matter to you, and you can see that with empathy. You are not perfect yourself either.

You have a free spirit

Condemning judgment is not your cup of tea: for you little is a matter of black and white and you are open to new ideas or other views. You see criticism as feedback (provided that it comes from someone to whom you are open) and although you have your own truths, you also realize that there is much more than one truth. And that you've probably never heard most of it, especially that.

You see life as a miracle

And that is an automatic consequence of the previous point. Because once you know that life is full of layers, views, ideas and starting points, there is still a lot to discover, investigate and understand. You can, therefore, enjoy nature intensely, and occasionally ask yourself deep questions about your existence and your role on this planet.

You are optimistic and realistic

Because although you realize very well that life can sometimes be disappointing and go through difficult times, you consciously opt for an optimistic approach to things. Even if that can be difficult for you, you assume that everything will change. And so it will return sooner or later for the better. You are therefore looking forward to what is yet to come, but you are prepared in the here and now for possible setbacks or difficulties if they arise.

You are flexible

Stubbornness is strange to you, and you are prepared to adapt to changing circumstances. You see unexpected developments as a part of life, and you keep your feet firmly on the ground while at the same time bending along with the change. That is the opposite of how an emotionally immature person would do: he stays with what he or she finds, while the rest has long since moved to another place.

You are resilient

Even if in your life the shit hits you, you remain calm and do not let yourself be overwhelmed. You try not to get compassion from others, or their condition when you are in conflict with someone, but you continue to walk independently on your chosen path and in the meantime take the hordes that you encounter. And you do that powerfully and without nagging. You like to keep yourself away from people who do that: it distracts, and it brings you the wrong energy.

You have patience

And so you know what hard work is, and that reaching your goal sometimes requires long marine time. You do not find hasty success because it is often ego-driven ('look how good I am!') And you understand that what you want is not always what life gives you at that moment. That patience is also expressed to people, and you are then able to forgive them if necessary. You do not project your own ideas on others or try to convince them that you are right, because you know that the other person has (has) led a very different life than you. And so he or she has to solve their own themes.

You are honest

And have no desire to cheat another, in short. Openness, honesty and clear communication are more important to you than fear of conflict. You are in harmony with yourself and feel no reason to lie or wear a mask. If only because that is especially very pleasant for yourself.

CPSIA information can be obtained
at www.ICGtesting.com
Printed in the USA
LVHW081609281020
670065LV00006B/191